# The
# ROLLER DERBY
# ATHLETE

## A skater's guide to fitness, training, strategy and nutrition

Ellen Parnavelas

BLOOMSBURY

LONDON · NEW DELHI · NEW YORK · SYDNEY

Published 2012 by Bloomsbury Publishing Plc, 50 Bedford Square,
London WC1B 3DP

Cover credits: Front: Whipity Pow jamming for the Dooms Daisies,
Rocky Mountain Rollergirls. Photo by Amanda Renee, Wicked
Shamrock Photography.
Back: Kamikaze Kitten jamming for Team England at the Roller
Derby World Cup 2011. Photo by Jason Ruffell.

ISBN (print) 978-1-4088-3239-4
ISBN (ePDF) 978-1-4081-8259-8
ISBN (ePUB) 978-1-4081-8260-4
A CIP catalogue record for this book is available from the British
Library

This book is produced using paper that is made from wood grown
in managed sustainable forests. It is natural, renewable and
recyclable. The logging and manufacturing processes conform to the
environmental regulations of the country of origin.

Commissioning Editor: Lisa Thomas
Design: Saffron Stocker

Printed in China by C&C Offset Printing Co Ltd.

10 9 8 7 6 5 4 3 2 1

Visit www.bloomsbury.com to find out more about our authors and
their books. You will find extracts, author interviews and our blog,
and you can sign up for newsletters to be the first to hear about our
latest releases and special offers.

# CONTENTS

# Foreword

In 2004 I joined a roller derby league. I didn't know what roller derby was. My team-mates didn't really know what roller derby was. We were a few girls in full protective gear learning to move in skates without falling at the jam skate session in the South Bronx in New York City. We were Gotham Girls Roller Derby and at the time we were one of just a few roller derby leagues to exist in the Unites States. Today – in 2012 – there are over 1,190 leagues in the US and throughout the world playing roller derby (www. derbyroster.com). If you had told me then that my life was about to change forever, I would have said, 'Whatever, I'm just here for a little exercise because I hate the gym and am a poor self-motivator.'

Roller derby has resurged in recent years with a big bang to join the 'alterna-sport' scene. America was a good place for roller derby to thrive. Tattoo shops were found in every city, even children's clothing was printed with skulls and guitars, and skateboarder Tony Hawk and snowboarder Sean White had become household names. Being safely different had become somewhat acceptable. So enter independently minded women looking for an organised group activity that wasn't volleyball at the YMCA. Hell, knitting was back and cool young women were doing it. What a great time to be alive!

To play roller derby in 2004, if you had a pulse and pair of skates, you were in. No experience was needed in either skating or athletics. It wasn't athleticism that brought us together. It did however require extreme dedication, a little blind faith and our good friend, the Internet. What is it that causes a person to just have no fear and decide to play a contact sport on a pair of roller skates of all things? I don't know what it is, but that little bit of 'crazy' is in every woman who plays roller derby.

Next came evolution. 'Back in the day' women chose clever 'derby' names and dressed in fishnet stockings and short skirts. As the sport grew we figured some things out. Fishnet burns your skin when you fall. It's more comfortable to sweat in a pair of athletic tights. Poorly made 'sexy' skirts ripped, fell apart, and had to go. We learned how to buy roller skates that actually fitted our feet from skater-owned businesses. We learned how to use wheels that worked for the different surfaces we played on instead of just picking our favourite colour. The names stayed, but as evolution dictates, the fittest survived, and we became fitter as we learned to be athletes. Our competitive instincts emerged and with every year we trained harder, faster and more seriously than before.

The first generation had passed, and growing pains began as we began to say goodbye to close team-mates who thought the new competitiveness and stricter athletic direction was not the same as the DIY fun they were strongly connected to. As time went on, we became exponentially more competitive and practice and fitness requirements were raised. We had become the misfits' old high school enemy, the athlete. And WE LOVED IT. I got great satisfaction from working out so hard I could barely walk, and I did it with a group of women who all were as addicted as I was. There is an immense camaraderie and satisfaction earned when you achieve new physical limits together. We feed off one another's energy and drive.

Today, roller derby is the core of my life. I have roller derby practice four days a week, every week including three hours of running, plyometrics and weights in addition to skating. Then there are efforts to get to yoga and speed skating on the other days of the week, body pain permitting. And if you're a roller derby athlete you are in pain daily. You learn to tell the difference between pain from a real injury versus the 'I play a contact sport' pain.

I think about roller derby as if it was a newly invented language, and I learned how to speak it in 2004. I have a lot of roller derby experience. I never skated before I joined a roller derby league, but it's been many years and I'm quite comfortable on wheels now. I get invited to travel to newer leagues and teach them about roller derby while still actively competing as part of a top-ranked international travelling team. Our sport is in a major growth trend where it's crucial that we foster its growth and offer education to newer leagues instead of being instant competitors with these new leagues as they form. So if 2012 is your first year skating, know that there are plenty of skaters who have been around a while and want to help you discover the same love of being an athlete playing roller derby that has kept us here all these years and hopefully for years to come.

*Suzy Hotrod*
*Gotham Girls Roller Derby*
*New York, NY*

Suzy Hotrod jamming for Team USA at the Roller Derby World Cup 2011.

# Introduction

Roller derby has been popular since the 1930s, but since 2001, it has experienced a major revival to become a very popular contemporary sport, with new leagues appearing all over the world at a rapid rate. Since 2001, roller derby has become a serious sport played by highly skilled and disciplined athletes. As the game itself has developed, the rules and strategy have evolved, as have the fitness and training practices of the skaters, taking the sport to a new level of athleticism.

Roller derby is popular for so many reasons. Not only does it help those that play it improve their general all-round fitness and increase their strength and stamina, it is a great way to combat stress caused by the frustrations of everyday life. It is also a fun and sociable way to exercise while meeting new people by participating in a team sport. Every roller derby league is a highly supportive community made up of a diverse and interesting range of individuals.

As a non-traditional team sport, it has attracted many people who have never previously played sports as well as experienced athletes. It is inclusive of people from a wide variety of sports backgrounds, from ice hockey and speed skating to netball, rugby, running, gymnastics and martial arts, as well as many first-time athletes.

Roller derby can be enjoyed by a wide range of individuals, as there are now men's and junior leagues, as well as recreational leagues for those who don't want to play at a highly competitive level.

Safety should always come first and roller derby is a demanding physical sport, so if you have any doubts about your health, it is advisable to check your health with your doctor before beginning to play.

## A little bit of roller derby history

- Roller derby first appeared in the 1930s as a sport for men and women based on the roller skating endurance races that had been growing in popularity since their origins in the 19th century.

- Roller derby has had many incarnations over the years and the rules are constantly evolving.

- In the 1970s, 80s and 90s, roller derby was shown on late night television in the US where sensationalist violence prevailed.

Male roller derby players in New York in 1931.

Members of the US roller skating team practising together at a Haringey rink for an upcoming UK roller derby in May 1953.

- Roller derby is now a legitimate competitive contact sport with a comprehensive set of rules to protect the safety of the players.

- There is no ball or stick involved in the game of roller derby.

- Roller derby has been undergoing a resurgence in popular culture, with numerous films, books and websites dedicated to the sport. It is also getting more and more coverage in the mainstream media.

- Men can and do play roller derby – there are even co-ed teams and leagues.

- Roller derby is not only played in the United States, there are now leagues all over the world.

This book is designed to focus on some basic principles that will help every roller derby skater. It explores the fitness elements involved in playing and training for roller derby. It shows you how to use on-skates agility training, plyometrics, core training, interval training and cross-training, all designed for building the muscles and enhancing the skills that power the roller derby athlete.

Knowing your sport and playing it well comes primarily from practice. However, knowing the basics of roller derby strategy will equip you with the tools you need to learn the game and be an effective player. This book explains some of the fundamentals of strategy as the game is played today, providing a great platform for the skater to build on.

A fundamental aspect of playing great roller derby is to know how to take care of your body and prepare it for playing a fast and furious contact sport on roller skates. This book looks at the potential risks involved in playing the sport and how to prepare your body for dealing with them, including stretching, preventing injuries and recovering from strenuous training.

In order to perform well as an athlete, the body must have the nutrition it requires. This book will help you understand what your body needs as fuel to play roller derby. It explains how your body produces energy and which sources of fuel the body uses to play roller derby, with advice on eating before, during and after training.

Atomatrix jamming for Oly Rollers' Cosa Nostra Donnas at the WFTDA Championships 2011.

# HOW TO USE THIS BOOK

## Chapter One: The game

Explains the fundamentals of how the sport is played, the different positions and how the game works. Introduces the different roller derby organisations, the various tournaments and competitions, gives a brief background to the history of roller derby and a summary of the people who are involved in playing the sport.

## Chapter Two: Strategy

Introduces the evolution of strategy with an article by veteran skater and international roller derby coach, Bonnie D. Stroir. Explains the differences between offence and defence and some of the other basic principles that the game is based on.

## Chapter Three: Fitness

Defines the different aspects that make up complete physical fitness and explores how each of these are used in playing roller derby, including cardiovascular fitness, muscular endurance, muscular strength, agility, speed, flexibility, balance and proprioception. Sets out the principles of which muscle groups are used and what demands are placed on the body in order to play the sport.

## Chapter Four: Training

Focuses on different types of training that will be beneficial for athletes training specifically for playing roller derby. Includes on-skates agility exercises with international roller derby coach Kamikaze Kitten, advice on interval training, practical exercises for strengthening core muscles, resistance and plyometric exercises and the benefits of cross-training using a range of other sports.

## Chapter Five: Looking after your body

Covers how to prepare the body for playing a physically demanding contact sport and maintain it in terms of preventing injury, stretching, joint care and recovery. Also explains some of the most common injuries that occur in playing roller derby with exercises to strengthen areas of weakness and help prevent them from happening.

## Chapter Six: Nutrition

Explores how an athlete requires the right diet to play at peak performance. Includes information on how best to fuel the body for playing roller derby and what to eat before, during and after training, as well as giving practical nutritional information for vegetarian and vegan athletes.

All the chapters feature interviews with skaters from all over the world who share their experiences and their practices as roller derby athletes – including direct quotes, practical advice, personal anecdotes and photos.

Tracy 'Disco' Akers skating for Team USA at the Roller Derby World Cup 2011.

# The game

# WHAT IS ROLLER DERBY?

Roller derby is a fast and furious contact sport played on roller skates. The sport has been present in various forms throughout the 20th century, but since 2001 it has experienced a major revival and become extremely popular. Now possibly 'the world's fastest growing sport', roller derby has become a truly global phenomenon with over 1,190 leagues now in existence throughout Europe, Asia, Australasia and the Americas. New leagues are forming all the time and it is not uncommon for crowds at games to reach several thousand spectators.

The speed at which the sport has developed is quite astounding as the current revival started in 2001 in Texas with just one league and yet over 1,190 leagues have formed since 2003. During this brief period, roller derby has changed and developed a lot and it is now regarded as a serious sport played by athletes. The rules of the game have evolved and become increasingly more established, and several organisations have been formed to regulate the sport and its practices.

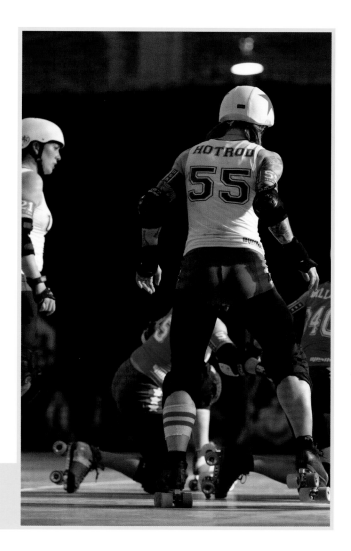

Suzy Hotrod on the jammer line for Team USA at the Roller Derby World Cup 2011.

# PLAYING ROLLER DERBY

Roller derby is played on an oval-shaped track by two teams of five players. In each team, four of the players are 'blockers' and one is the 'jammer'. The blockers from both teams skate around the track together, forming a 'pack', with the two jammers starting behind them. The jammer is a skater whose job it is to race through the pack and lap the players on the opposing team, scoring points for passing the opposing players. The blockers in the pack try to stop the opposing jammer from getting through the pack while also trying to help their own jammer through by blocking the opposing blockers.

The jammers race through the pack once, at which time no points are scored but the jammer that gets through the pack first is awarded a 'lead jammer status', giving her the advantage of being able to 'call off' the jam. The jammers score a point for every opposing blocker they pass from their second lap onwards, as long as they pass each player in bounds and without getting any penalties.

The jammers may continue to race and score points for up to two minutes, or until the 'lead jammer' calls off the jam. The jammer scores four points each time she gets through the pack and passes all four opposing blockers. She can score an additional point per pass if she laps the opposing jammer as well.

Roller derby games are known as 'bouts' and are made up of two 30-minute periods with a half-time break. Each period is made up of 'jams' of up to two minutes. There is no limit to the number of jams that can take place in each period but the period ends after 30 minutes when the last jam reaches its natural conclusion. When the lead jammer calls off the jam or the two-minute period ends, play stops and the officials calculate the score. The team with the most points at the end of the game wins.

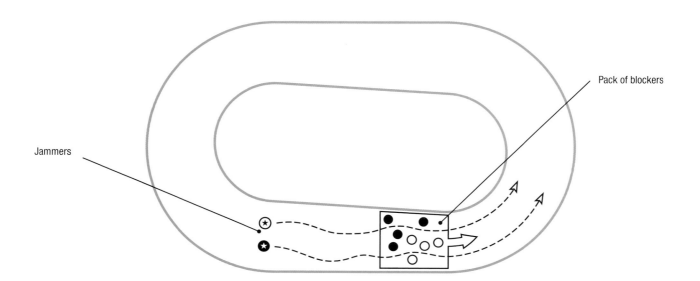

Pack of blockers

Jammers

# THE TRACK

Roller derby can be played on either a flat or a banked track with different leagues favouring one or the other. Historically, it was played more often on a banked track as this added to the speed, the drama and the spectacle of the game. In recent years, flat tracks have been favoured as they are both more convenient and accessible.

Most leagues today play roller derby on a flat track measured according to the official WFTDA measurements that can be found at **http://wftda. com/rules**. Banked tracks also have a standardised set of dimensions, and these were adapted to create the flat track measurements at the beginning of the current roller derby revival in 2001. Flat track roller derby can be played on any clean, flat surface including polished wood, concrete or indoor sports court floors. The track must be clearly demarcated by a raised boundary that is clearly visible to all skaters and referees.

## Penalties

Penalties are signalled and enforced by the referees as they occur during a bout. A penalty is given to a skater during gameplay for breaking the rules or committing a foul and involves the individual being excluded from the game for a specific period of time, leaving her team in a position of disadvantage.

## Penalty box

In every bout there is a designated 'penalty box' set up for skaters who are sent off for penalties. This is a seated area outside of the track. Skaters must enter the penalty box by skating in an anticlockwise direction and must re-enter the track behind all the other skaters in the pack once the penalty time has been served.

## Rules

Roller derby is played according to a vast set of complicated rules, which are slightly varied for play on flat or banked tracks. The rules are designed to make the sport as safe as possible for the players while maintaining its 'contact' element. Some of the essential rules can be summarised as follows:

- Blocking is legal but there are restrictions on how it can be executed – players cannot grab, pull or trip one another, for example.
- Falling deliberately in front of another skater is prohibited.
- There are comprehensive rules defining 'blocking zones', meaning the parts of the body used by the skater performing a block, for example, no use of fully extended arms for blocking.
- There are comprehensive rules defining 'target zones' for blocking, meaning the parts of the body

The penalty box is a designated seated area outside of the track where skaters who have been sent off for penalties must remain until their penalty time has been served.

a skater can initiate contact with when executing a block, for example, no blocking to the back, below the knee or above the shoulder.

- Only skaters who are 'in play' can engage another skater to impede their movement on the track.
- Only skaters who are moving in an anticlockwise direction are able to block other skaters. Blocking when stationary or moving in a clockwise direction is prohibited.
- Skaters must have at least one foot on the track when executing a block.
- If a skater is blocked and knocked off the track, she must re-enter the track behind the skater that initiated the block so she does not gain an unfair advantage in relative position.
- Jammers do not receive a point if they are out of bounds or foul the player they are passing.

Other rules govern all players' conduct during the bout. Breaking any of these rules can lead to players being sent off for penalties, and, as a result of that, spending time in the penalty box. Players usually spend a minute in the penalty box for one major penalty. This may not sound like much time, but a minute can be an entire jam. An accumulation of major penalties can also lead to expulsion from the game.

A much more detailed outline of the most commonly used set of rules for playing flat track roller derby can be found on the WFTDA website at **http://wftda.com/rules**.

In roller derby, referees are responsible for enforcing the rules to protect the safety of the skaters.

# POSITIONS IN ROLLER DERBY

Roller derby is played by two teams of five players. One of the players on each team is the 'jammer', and the other four players on each team are blockers. One of the blockers on each team also acts as a 'pivot'. The blockers and pivots skate together in a pack, and the jammers start each jam skating behind them. There are ten players on the track in any one jam, unless any of the players has been sent to the penalty box.

In a bout, each team will usually have up to 20 players, with up to 14 on the roster for a specific bout on their bench so that they can alternate the line-ups of players that go on in each jam to prevent the players from getting too exhausted. Each jam of up to two minutes can be very intense and physically demanding, especially for the jammers. Leagues can change a teams' roster from one game to the next.

## The pack

The pack is defined by the largest group of blockers from both teams skating in bounds and within no more than 10 feet in front of or behind the nearest pack skater. The jammer is not part of the pack.

The pack: Team Sweden and Team Brasil at the Roller Derby World Cup 2011.

## Jammer

The jammer is a racing skater whose job is to sprint through the pack and score points for her team by lapping the players on the opposing team. The second time the jammer gets through the pack she can score one point for every opposition player passed in the pack and one point for lapping the opposing jammer, as long as the jammer passes them legally and in bounds. Both jammers can score points on their second time through the pack but the jammer who breaks through the pack first is called the 'lead jammer'. The lead jammer is able to 'call off' the jam whenever she chooses by putting her hands on her hips and can use this to her team's advantage to prevent the other team from scoring points. The jammers are recognisable because they wear helmet covers with a star on each side, also known as 'jammer panties'.

Second Hand Smoke jamming for Minnesota RollerGirls against Texas Rollergirls' Texecutioners at the WFTDA Championships

## Blockers

In addition to the pivot (see facing page), each team has three blockers on the track. The blockers are there to prevent the opposing jammer from getting through the pack and scoring points. They are also there to help their jammer get through the pack by stopping the opposing blockers from hitting their jammer off the track or getting in her way. Blockers play offensively or defensively depending on the situation during the game. They must be adaptable and able to change positions to ensure that they are helping their team at all times. Blockers line up in front of the jammers at the start of a jam. They play a key role in determining the speed of the pack and keeping the pack formed.

Atomatrix jamming for Team USA approaches a strong wall of Team Canada blockers at the Roller Derby World Cup 2011.

## Pivot

The pivot's role is to be the pace setter for the pack – to slow them down or speed them up – and direct the blockers on her team to where they need to be. The other skaters look to the pivot for guidance. The pivots are designated by wearing a helmet cover with a vertical stripe down the centre, also known as a 'pivot panty'. The pivots are able to take on the position of jammer if their team's jammer is finding it difficult to get through the pack. In this situation, the jammer will pass her helmet cover to the pivot who will then become the jammer for that team. This is a strategic move known as 'passing the star'.

Ninjette pivoting for Team England at the Roller Derby World Cup 2011.

Ruby Ribcrusher pivoting for Team Australia at the Roller Derby World Cup 2011.

# REFEREES AND OTHER SUPPORTING CREW

The referees' job in roller derby is the same as in other sports: to make sure everyone remains safe and plays by the rules. The rules of roller derby are very complex with many different nuances for different situations. The game is often played so fast that it is difficult for the skaters to know whether they have committed an offence, even if they are very familiar with the rules. There may be disputes but the referees' word is always final.

In order to ensure the safety of the skaters, the referees have several duties to fulfil, the first of which is to make sure all skaters are fully protected with all the essential safety equipment, that this equipment is in good condition and that it fits correctly. At the beginning of any bout, all the skaters in both teams line up to have their equipment checked by the referees. If the referees find that a skater is missing any part of her kit, or that it doesn't fit, she will not be able to compete in the bout. Their other duties include counting points scored by each jammer; keeping track of the timings for each jam and the overall game clocks; communicating with the announcers, scorekeepers and team captains; calling out penalties; and stopping the game in case of injury.

In a bout or any scrimmage situation, referees will give players penalties for committing fouls during the game. A major penalty results in the offending skater being sent to the penalty box, after which she can re-enter the pack behind all the other skaters who are playing in that jam.

With multiple players making full contact at any given time, it would be impossible for one referee to be able to keep an eye on all the skaters simultaneously. There are several different types of referee in roller derby, because in this fast-paced sport there are too many jobs for one referee to do alone. Indeed, there can be up to seven referees on duty in a given bout.

In roller derby, the referees have their own unique derby names and numbers, as do the skaters.

## Jammer referees

In a roller derby bout, there is always one referee watching each jammer closely. They watch from the inside of the track and signify who is the lead jammer, that is, the jammer who breaks through the pack first. The jammer referees count the number of points their jammer is scoring. They must keep a close eye on any penalties committed by their jammer and ultimately keep the players safe.

Cherry Fury refereeing at the Roller Derby World Cup 2011. Referees are vital to the game of roller derby to protect the safety of the skaters.

## Pack referees

The pack referees watch from both the inside and outside of the track. Their job is to keep an eye on the main pack skaters, watching out for any penalties. There are usually four pack referees watching the jam at all times to enforce any necessary penalties for infringements of the rules.

## Head referee

The head referee has the last word on all situations and the final say in disputes. He or she instructs the other referees and assigns each referee's role.

## NSOs

In addition to the referees, there are also at least six NSOs or non-skating officials. The NSOs help referees to coordinate the game, and they too have a variety of different jobs to do off the track. The NSOs include scorekeepers who are informed by the jammer referees of the number of points scored in each jam, and keep track of the total scores throughout the game. They share this information with the scoreboard operator, who communicates it to the audience on either a digital or a manual scoreboard, depending on the venue.

The NSOs are also in charge of the penalty box. They include penalty timers whose job it is to make sure skaters in the penalty box serve the correct amount of time. The penalty trackers are responsible for keeping count of how many penalties each player has been given.

## Other supporting crew

There is a whole host of other supporting crew involved in roller derby leagues without whom bout situations would be a lot less entertaining. Announcers provide live commentary for the audiences at games; there is half-time entertainment in the form of DJs, bands, dancers or cheerleaders; then there are the coaches; and, of course, the all-important fans complete the picture of roller derby as a spectator sport today.

# BACKGROUND TO THE ROLLER DERBY REVIVAL

Roller derby has been around in various forms since the early 1930s but the current revival started in Austin, Texas in 2001.

A member of the alternative music scene known as Devil Dan, later to be revealed as musician Daniel Eduardo Policarpo, had the idea of launching a roller derby for the women of Austin. His idea was very popular and, by early 2001, he had signed up about twenty women to participate.

Devil Dan devised four teams: the Rhinestone Cowgirls, captained by Anya Jack, aka Hot Lips Dolly; the Holy Rollers, captained by Amanda Harrison, aka Miss Information; the Putas del Fuego, captained by April Ritzenhaler, aka La Muerta; and the Hellcats, captained by Nancy Haggarty, aka Iron Maiden.

According to the fable, Devil Dan suddenly disappeared and the newly appointed captains of the teams took it upon themselves to get organised. Nicknamed the SheEOs, this group of women got into gear and started up the first female flat track roller derby league. They formed Bad Girl Good Woman Productions, and pooling their skills they taught each other's recruits how to skate, play the game and get themselves physically ready for the athleticism of the sport. Sparkle Plenty captained the rules committee and together they devised a new set of rules for women's flat track roller derby.

These women had started up the first DIY women-only roller derby league, and by early 2002, the league had 45 players all of whom had volunteered to help run different parts of it, establishing the tradition of the skaters operating the league themselves. They played their first bout in June 2002.

In early 2003, Bad Girl Good Woman productions split into two leagues: the Texas Rollergirls and the TXRD Lonestar Rollergirls. Not long after, it became apparent that the dream of grassroots women's roller derby was not confined to the city limits of Austin, Texas. In 2003 Denise Grimes, aka Ivanna S. Pankin,

a painter from the punk scene in Phoenix Arizona, started work on forming the Arizona Roller Derby. Nearby, in the town of Tuscon, a former truck-stop waitress who was to become Kim Sin heard about the Arizona Roller Derby and decided to start her own league, which held its first rollergirl recruitment meeting in December 2003. In April 2004 Tucson Roller Derby played their first bout against Arizona Roller Derby.

Since 2003 roller derby leagues have sprung up at a pace that is as fast and furious as the sport itself. In Brooklyn, New York, Karin Bruce, aka Chassis Crass, started up the Gotham Girls Roller Derby. Celia Fate started up the Carolina Rollegirls, who were soon followed by the Rat City Rollergirls of Seattle, the Kansas City Roller Warriors, the Mad Rollin' Dolls in Wisconsin, the Rose City Rollers in Portland, the Rocky Mountain Rollergirls in Denver, the Bay Area Rollergirls in San Francisco, the Minnesota Rollergirls in Minneapolis and the Providence Rollergirls in Rhode Island.

There are now men's and women's leagues all over the world from the North Pole to Singapore, New Zealand to Argentina and Finland, and the sport is still rapidly growing in popularity.

Gotham Girls' All-Stars skate out at the WFTDA Championships 2011.

# ROLLER DERBY ORGANISATIONS

In 2004, the United Leagues Coalition, or ULC, was formed to establish a cohesive governing body for women's flat track roller derby charged with the responsibility of drawing up a standardised set of rules and organising competitions between leagues. Beginning with a mission statement promising to facilitate the development of athletic ability, sportswomanship and goodwill among member leagues, according to their website, their governing philosophy is 'By the skaters, for the skaters'.

The ULC held their first meeting in 2005, welcoming any leagues that wanted to join. This led 30 leagues to join forces, and at the same time the decision was taken to rename the organisation the Women's Flat Track Derby Association (now known as WFTDA), the organisation at the head of the sport today.

WFTDA is now the central governing body behind women's flat track roller derby. WFTDA is responsible for setting the rules of the game, establishing safety guidelines and organising officially sanctioned competitions among members. Annual championship games are held based on these competitions, while a ranking system of member leagues has also been established. In September 2006 the WFTDA opened its doors to new members and has continued to do so ever since.

The WFTDA member leagues are divided into four regions: US East, US West, US North Central and US South Central. Two new regions, Canada and Europe, have recently been formed due to the rapid growth of roller derby outside the US. These regions have yet to be developed, and until they establish more members' teams in those regions will compete in their closest US region for rankings and tournaments.

Gotham Girls' All-Stars skate out at the WFTDA Championships 2011.

Although WFTDA is the most established governing body in the sport today, there are many leagues operating and competing that are not members of WFTDA. For instance, there are several other organisations that have recently been established for other forms of roller derby. The Men's Roller Derby Association, MRDA, was established for the increasing number of male leagues and teams that have started up in recent years. The Old School Derby Association, OSDA, was started in 2007 for a version of roller derby based on earlier forms of the game played predominantly on a banked track, though this organisation caters to men's, women's and mixed-sex groups playing on flat or banked tracks. The OSDA Professional League established its first team in 2010, playing on a banked track. The major banked-track leagues formed the World Organisation of Roller Derby, WORD, in 2009, with rules compatible with those of WFTDA.

## Rankings and tournaments

Every year, the WFTDA holds tournaments involving the top 10 WFTDA teams from each region. The three top teams in each region then go through to compete in the annual WFTDA Championships.

There are a number of other tournaments held every year by WFTDA, non-WFTDA and banked track roller derby organisations. For example, the Chicago Invitational that was held in 2011 – the first banked-track tournament played between both flat and banked-track organisations with large sums of prize money up for grabs.

2011 was a particularly exciting year for roller derby as it witnessed the first-ever Roller Derby World Cup, where the very best players from Argentina, Australia, Brazil, Canada, England, Finland, France, Germany, Ireland, New Zealand, Scotland, Sweden and the USA represented their countries in a global tournament held in Toronto, Canada. As roller derby continues to grow, there are likely to be many more international tournaments held every year.

Suzy Hotrod and Deranged flying the American flag at the Roller Derby World Cup 2011.

# WHO PLAYS ROLLER DERBY?

Roller derby has always been played by both men and women, but in recent years, women have paved the way for the current revival and made the sport their own. Part of roller derby's appeal is that it is the first contact sport to be been developed by women for women. More and more men have started playing roller derby with men's teams and leagues also forming at a rapid rate, however, the sport continues to be led by women with men following in their footsteps.

Since 2001, roller derby has been a female-dominated sport. However, men have always been involved in the roller derby revival, often in supporting roles such as refereeing or as other non-skating officials as these roles can be taken on by males or females even if the league they belong to is a women's league.

Men, women and children play roller derby today. Many junior roller derby leagues have been started in recent years so that children and teenagers under the age of 18 are able to play roller derby. Most junior roller derby leagues are based in the US, however there are now a few in the UK as junior roller derby becomes more popular.

Men's roller derby, or 'merby' as it is now known, began in 2006 with the launch of Pioneer Valley Roller Derby in Northampton, Massachusetts. When Sarah Lang, aka Pink Panza, and her boyfriend Jake Fahy, aka Bazooka Joe, started up the league, they decided to establish teams for both men and women. The first men's team was called the Dirty Dozen. Their first public scrimmage was organised by Justice Feelgood Marshall, a referee for Charm City Roller Girls, and it took place at half-time during the Charm City bout. Justice Feelgood Marshall went on to form Harm City Homicide in 2007, and other new leagues for me quickly followed, led by the New York Shock Exchange and the Death Quads of Connecticut.

In 2007 these leagues formed the Men's Derby Coalition, now known as the Men's Roller Derby Association, to create a community for male derby skaters and to share resources and knowledge from their collective experiences. On their website, the MRDA promise 'to foster the development of sustainable roller derby leagues, to cultivate positive sportsmanship on and off the track, and to enhance the derby community' as well as providing 'new leagues with direction and encouragement while offering strategic benefits to member leagues'.

As with WFTDA, all the member leagues in the MRDA are skater-owned and operated and have a say in the development of the organisation's policies.

Man Shaped Dog of Tyne & Fear blocks Lil Joker of Manchester Roller Derby.

The MRDA maintains standards for rules, safety and gameplay for local, regional and international competitions. With the support of WFTDA, the MRDA aims to build a similarly influential brother organisation for men's roller derby leagues.

New men's teams and leagues are forming all the time. Men's leagues in the US, Europe and Australia have multiplied in recent years, with men's roller derby becoming increasingly international as the sport grows.

## Roller derby is more than just a sport

Whether played by men or women, roller derby is a culture that embraces all athletic backgrounds and abilities. The motto of the WFTDA best sums up the spirit of it: 'Real, Strong, Athletic, Revolutionary'. It is a culture within which women and increasing numbers of men learn, develop, achieve and express themselves through the medium of sport – but there is far more to it than that.

Roller derby isn't just a sport; it's a way of life. For those who play, it reaches into every aspect of their lives, from social life to diet to politics and personal relationships. Every league provides a unique community within which to train and play the sport. There is a place for everyone in roller derby, as it embraces people from all backgrounds, from lifelong athletes to first-time sports lovers. As the sport has grown and developed, a greater emphasis has been placed on its athleticism, and there is a lot of discussion at the moment as to whether the sport will be played professionally in the coming years.

Team Scotland huddle at the Roller Derby World Cup 2011.

# Strategy

# AN EVOLVING RULEBOOK

Roller derby is, in many ways, still in its infancy and is growing and evolving all the time. Since the first shared rule set was established by the WFTDA in 2005, the sport has gone through many growing pains and revisions. In its current form, the rules of flat track roller derby have been developed into a concise yet detailed set of guidelines. However, these will inevitably be subject to small changes as the game becomes further developed in the future. As the rules have changed, so has the strategy for gameplay within these rules.

In any sport, strategy can be summed up as ways in which the members of a team work together to achieve a common goal, inevitably, winning the game. In playing roller derby, this is very much the same. As roller derby has evolved, a set of subtle and complex rules has evolved and continues to evolve and as it does, so does the strategy used for gameplay. As roller derby strategy is constantly changing with new trends appearing all the time, it is difficult to explain or give particular recommendations. However, there are some principles of basic strategy that should be understood.

When thinking about strategy, the most important thing to bear in mind is the WFTDA rule 2.2.2 which states that 'the team with the most points at the end of a game wins'. This forms the root of all strategy which is to score points and stop the opposing team from scoring.

In the previous chapter, the basics of the game were explained. The main object to aim for in any game situation is helping your jammer get through the pack as quickly and easily as possible, ideally gaining lead jammer status on the way through, while stopping the opposing jammer from getting through the pack or scoring any points.

There are different styles of gameplay that can be used to achieve each of these ends. The blockers and pivot in the pack, and to some extent the jammer, can work together to use the pack position to their advantage. Every jam creates a new two-minute opportunity to gain control of the pack and take advantage of your opponents' weaknesses and then exploit those weaknesses quickly to gain a competitive advantage.

# THE EVOLUTION OF STRATEGY IN ROLLER DERBY
## BY BONNIE D. STROIR

At the first tournament in roller derby's revival, I remember sitting in the audience and telling some of my team-mates, 'Look at that … they're controlling the front of the pack! Genius strategy!' And it was, at the time. Now teams who can control the back of the pack think they're pretty cutting edge. And they are. Until the front of the pack becomes the dominant place again, I suppose.

A set of athletes working together towards a common goal is the most fundamental principle of strategy, in every sport, perhaps. But the development of this 'front wall' was the first time we'd really seen it in roller derby.

### In the beginning
In the early days, there was much more sensationalism in roller derby than there is now. Skaters often still debate 'is this show or is this sport?' to anyone who will listen, but the truth is, the debate really ended back in 2006 when 'skate fast, hit hard and turn left' wasn't enough to win games any more. No matter how much anyone wanted to 'just have fun' (as is often said), after a while … everyone hates losing!

Every woman in the world has at least a hundred competitive bones in her body. So even the die-hard party chicks in the sport will concede to doing what it takes to win after a spirit-crushing number of ass-beatings.

So strategy began to take hold of roller derby, little by little. Many of the early, staple strategies of the sport came from Arizona Roller Derby's coach Pauly, who now lives in Canada. He coined the well-known derby terms 'live' and 'dead' points, 'waterfalling' and 'goading', (which, for reasons unknown, skaters started referring to as 'goating'. It's like a strategic game of telephone!)

Another coach from Arizona, Pitchit, champions the theory known as 'Default Strategy', with an easy-to-read graph that basically states: 'If your jammer is X, do Y. If the opposing jammer is Y, do X'.

### Finding the loopholes
For many teams, their strategy in roller derby involves finding loopholes in the ruleset to exploit. This keeps volunteer referees on their toes and, for a little while, can stun the opposing team into inaction. At least, until they figure out how to answer it. The sport is new enough, still, that you can shock the opposition simply by having a greater understanding of the rules.

I call these 'trend strategies' because as soon as the element of surprise is gone, often so is the novelty of bothering to make the effort. A strategy such as a pivot lying on the ground with one finger on the jammer line, just to pull a power trip on the opposing team, who then question whether or not they need to be behind her hips to proceed with the jam? Total trend strategy. Skaters 10 years from now probably won't bother.

### Firming up strategy
Some seeming trend strategies, however, become staples of the game for practical purposes.

Strategy in roller derby has come a long way from 'hold the front' being the only play anyone had ever seen (outside of the bash-n-smash as it was in the beginning). A blocker's mental soundtrack is typically a little more sophisticated than 'Me hit jammer' in more experienced teams. There are all kinds of psychological warfare being played in today's games. Everything from face make-up on some skaters to facial expressions to bodily odours can be seen as a way to gain an advantage.

### *The future of strategy*

We still have a way to go. Even as a strategy coach, who lives for the thrill of surprising an opposing team with awesome new tricks, a part of me still kind of looks forward to the day when roller derby is so much more established, like basketball or football is in America. A time when the game has moved past gimmicks and trends in the exploitation of the rules, and matured past the point where players are prepared to use psychological cheap shots.

When the game becomes completely about which team has a dominant understanding of technique, that's when it will develop an undying fan base that spans far beyond our inner circles.

Because when there's nothing new under the sun anymore and the game is understood by everyone to be as evolved as it's ever going to be, then it becomes a true war of attrition. Skill versus skill, execution versus execution. Not so much with surprises, as who was the better team of skaters that day. That's when the sport will have moved past its teenage years and into a real age of focus and driven purpose.

For now, we're a sport in its adolescence. The spirit is strong, but the will is not yet consistent. The passion is enough to change the world, but not entirely well channelled yet. And our evolution in strategy completely reflects our maturing with time. Still, it's a very exciting, explosive and fascinating time to be a skater, coach or anyone in any way involved with

such a crazy movement of diverse people with nothing less than the potential to change the face, feet and thighs of women's sports.

# SKATER PROFILE: *BONNIE D. STROIR, SAN DIEGO DERBY DOLLS, CALIFORNIA, USA*

**How long have you been playing roller derby?**
I started in October 2003.

**Did you skate before you played roller derby?**
Not in any formal or consistent capacity. Just occasional rink sessions and skating outside sometimes.

**Did you play any other sports before you started roller derby?**
There was a lot of soccer in my childhood, but I quit in the 10th grade because I wanted to work more hours at my job.

**What additional off-skates training do you do and how often?**
I can't do anything consistent, or I get bored. So it's literally something different every day. It could be swimming, jump rope, power walking, calisthenics, yoga … I just need as much variety as possible.

**Which other sports support roller derby?**
I feel like I learn something every time I play or watch any sport in the world, and bring it back to roller derby.

**What type of training has helped you to improve most as a skater?**
Just being in love with roller skating. The off-skates workouts I have to force. There's no part of me that willingly puts on running shoes: it's a fight. But skating, I love. Skating I can and (often will) spend all day just being on skates for no reason at all. I love rolling, and seeing what kinds of funky things I can do while I'm rolling … and I think that's why my agility is pretty bangin'.

**What advice would you give new skaters about training for roller derby?**
Do the stretching, do the weight training. If you don't, you'll have to stop because your body can't support what you're trying to do, when you finally get to a high level. Think long-term, and start training for that now!

**How has roller derby affected your lifestyle?**
I've been in it since I was 22, so I've pretty much gone from a girl to a woman in roller derby. There's no part of my life that it has not affected. From leadership to physical and emotional endurance … roller derby's been my sport, my college and my finishing school.

**How is roller derby is progressing as a sport?**
It's coming a little closer to my goal of being professional, every day.

**What does the future holds for roller derby as a sport?**
There are a lot of futures for the sport, not just one. Some will play professionally, some will play as amateurs and others recreationally. When it becomes professional for some, others will benefit with more local sponsors and skating rinks being built. The sport will become more accessible to women and kids in low-income areas. That is really important to me, personally. And for everyone who likes things exactly as they are right now, I believe this level of competition will always be available too. One future doesn't have to cancel out any others, in my opinion. They only help each other. The future is pretty bright!

# BASIC STRATEGY FOR GAME PLAY

The blockers in the pack can choose to play offensively or defensively at any given time during each jam of up to two minutes. Before the start of each jam, the team will decide which skaters will be responsible for playing the different roles in the pack. These roles can be clearly divided into 'offence' and 'defence'.

### Offence and defence

However, as the situation can change very quickly, it is advantageous for the skaters in the pack to be able to change their position and strategy to adapt to the constantly changing conditions of the game. In roller derby, offence and defence are often played at the same time because each team is trying to help their jammer get through the pack and score points while preventing the opposing jammer from doing so.

### Offence

Offensive game play can be defined as the following:

* Helping your jammer to complete her initial pass and subsequent scoring passes.
* Actively moving or blocking the opposing blockers to clear safe and clear paths for your jammer, also known as 'friendly sides'.
* Helping your jammer to score points.
* Providing other assistance to your jammer such as whips and pushes to help her through the pack.
* Disabling any opposing players that pose a potential threat to your jammer.
* Breaking up any walls formed by the opposing blockers to prevent your jammer from getting through the pack and scoring points.
* Slowing down the speed of the pack so that it is easier for your jammer to get through the pack and score points.
* Trapping a blocker from the opposing team to gain control over the speed of the pack.

Team Australia's Muzzarati goes in to break up Team England's wall at the Roller Derby World Cup 2011.

## Defence

Defensive game play can be defined as follows:

- Preventing the opposing jammer from getting through the pack and scoring points.
- Speeding up the pack if the opposing jammer is the lead jammer to make it more difficult for her to lap the pack and score points.
- Getting all your skaters to skate at the front of the pack if the opposing jammer is leading so that it is more difficult for the opposing jammer to get past them and therefore score points.
- Making walls to hold back the opposing jammer and prevent her from scoring points.

Team Canada's Bone Machine blocks Team France's jammer Kozmic Bruise to prevent her from getting through the pack.

## Blocking

Blocking can be done in different ways but essentially, it just means getting in the way of the members of the opposing team and preventing them from scoring points. It must be done legally, in bounds and within the engagement zone or will result in penalties. Different types of blocking are positional blocking, which means impeding another skater's movement on the track without using contact; hitting or making contact with the legal target contact zones to knock an opposing skater down or out of bounds; or making walls to impede a skater's movement on the track. A detailed set of rules for blocking can be found in the rules document of the WFTDA website.

## Man on

This is an offensive strategy that is employed when a jammer is the only jammer in the pack whereby all the blockers pick a blocker each from the opposing team and focus on blocking the opposing blocker to prevent them from making walls or engaging the jammer, leaving her free to pass through the pack unobstructed.

Helsinki's pivot Estrogeena Davis engages in some offensive blocking on Leeds Roller Dolls' pivot Venus De Pileup.

Team Canada's Smack Daddy blocks Kamikaze Kitten jamming for Team England at the Roller Derby World Cup 2011.

## Jamming

Jamming can be just as tactical and strategy-focused as blocking. An effective jammer will always be one step ahead of the game, knowing where the opposing jammer is at all times and able to second-guess the strategies that the blockers of the opposing team will try to employ. As well as sprinting, juking, jumping, using quick lateral movements, stopping or accelerating suddenly, changing direction and doing anything in her power to get through the pack and score points without getting sent off for major penalties, there are a few strategic things a jammer can also do to ensure that her team scores as many points as possible and prevent the other team from scoring. The most effective way to do this is to gain lead jammer status and thereby the advantage of being able to choose when to call off the jam. Calling off the jam at the right moment is an essential part of strategy for jammers. A jammer can also prevent the opposing jammer from getting to be lead jammer by knocking her out of bounds off the start line and before she has entered the engagement zone. That way, she cannot get lead even if she is the first jammer out of the pack. Jammers can engage each other anywhere on the track so can block each other wherever necessary to impede the opposing jammer's progress.

Suzy Hotrod jumps the apex jamming for Team USA at the Roller Derby World Cup 2011.

## Defining the pack and the engagement zone

In order to put some of the basic principles of roller derby strategy into play, it is important to understand the rules of the game, especially those defining the pack and the engagement zone. Without understanding these basic principles, it is very difficult to effectively manipulate the pack to your team's advantage.

The pack is defined by the largest group of blockers from both teams skating in bounds, within proximity. This means within 10 feet in front of or behind the nearest pack skater. The jammer is not considered to be part of the pack. The pack is made up of blockers.

The engagement zone is the area in which the jammer may be engaged by a blocker. It is the area on the track where skaters are considered to be in play, and extends 20 feet from the front of the pack to 20 feet from the back of the pack. When a blocker is outside of the engagement zone, she is considered to be out of play. Skaters who are out of play may not block the opposing jammer or any of the opposing blockers. They are also prohibited from assisting any of their own team-mates, including their jammer.

**Out of play**

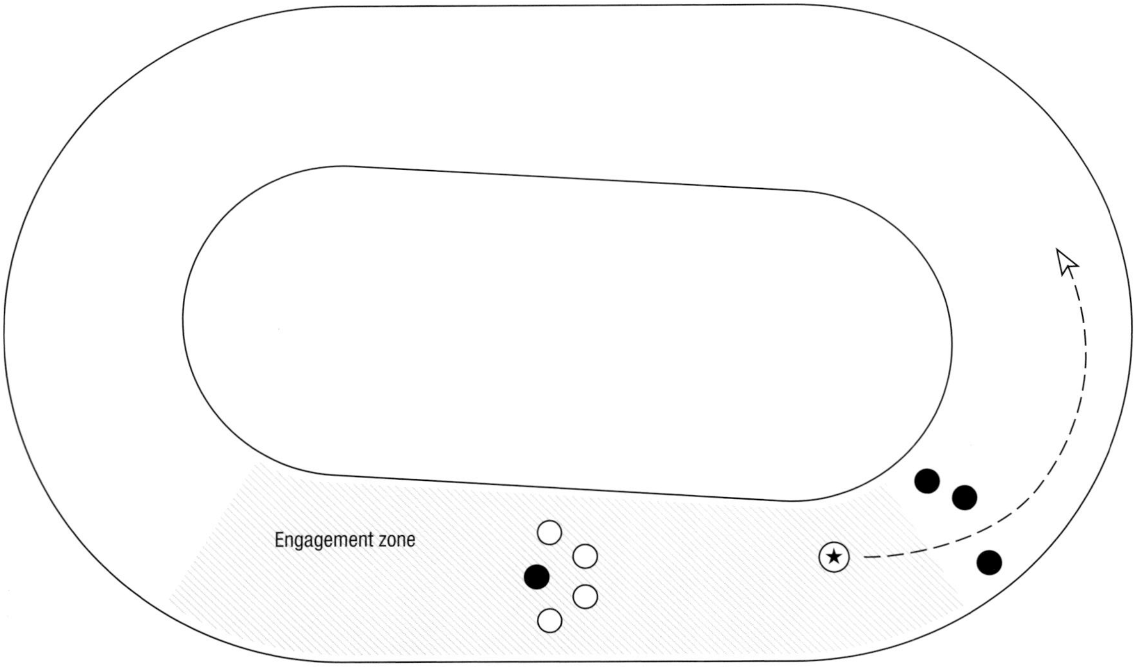

Engagement zone

Blocker held behind
team mates

'Out of play' blockers not allowed
to block jammer

## Slowing down or speeding up the pack

Controlling the speed of the pack can have a big impact on your own and the other team's ability to score points. If your jammer is lead jammer or the opposing jammer is in the penalty box, ideally you want to slow down the pack so that it is easier for your jammer to get through and score points. If the opposing jammer is lead jammer or your jammer is in the penalty box, you want to speed up the pack to prevent the opposing jammer from getting though the pack and scoring points. To do so, your skaters must skate as fast as they can while still remaining part of the pack.

Team USA's blockers at the front of the pack to make it more difficult for Team Canada's jammer to get past them and score points.

## Bridging

Bridging is when you spread your team-mates out around the track within 10 feet of each other in order to extend the pack as far as possible. This is a useful method that can be used for a number of different purposes. Bridging enables your team to allow their blockers to cover a greater distance on the track and still remain within the engagement zone without causing a 'no pack' situation or going out of play. It also enables blockers at the front to chase the jammer out of the front of the pack for a greater distance without going out of play or getting penalties for destroying the pack. Or, to knock the jammer out of bounds and then skate backwards so that she has to re-enter as far behind the pack as possible. In order for this tactic to work effectively, communication is vital. It can only work if all four blockers are communicating and working together.

One of Oly Rollers' blockers falls back to bridge to keep her two team-mates at the front of the pack in play so they can block Gotham's jammer Bonnie Thunders from getting through and scoring.

### Trapping an opposing blocker or 'goating'

'Goating' means trapping a blocker from the opposing team behind your blockers in order to control the speed and location of the pack. Because the pack is defined as the largest group of blockers from both teams skating within proximity, the team who have trapped an opposing blocker will be able to control the pack speed. This tactic is most commonly used to slow down the pack, making it easier for the jammer to get past and to gain control over the distance of the engagement zone in which the opposing team are able to block the jammer without going out of play.

This tactic is most effective when a jammer is leading and is approaching the pack well ahead of the opposing jammer, or as a way to react when a jammer is stuck behind a wall of opposing blockers at the front of the pack. In this situation, if the team traps an opposing blocker at the back of the pack and slows down the speed of the pack, the opposing blockers in the wall in front are likely to go out of play. They must then let the jammer past or be penalised. This tactic must be executed with caution or the team will risk being penalised for destroying the pack.

Southern Discomfort men's roller derby practise trapping an opposing blocker to control the speed of the pack.

## Starts: fast or slow?

Different strategies can be used in different situations to get the jam started as quickly or slowly as possible. Both types of start can be used to a team's advantage in different situations.

### Slow start

Starting the jam off slowly is often used as a strategy to kill time when the jammer or any of the team's blockers are in the penalty box so that they can catch up to the pack quickly once they are released. It is also used when the team is at an advantage in terms of points in order to run the time down on the clock to protect those points. There are risks involved in employing this tactic, as having a slow pack will make it easier for the opposing jammer to get

through in one swift motion, so it is not appropriate in every situation.

### Taking a knee/fast starts

In the past, this tactic has most often been employed in a power jam situation by the team in a position of advantage with their jammer as the only jammer on the track. If all the blockers in that team take a knee as soon as the pack whistle goes, the referees will declare that there is 'no pack' enabling the jammers to be released immediately. More recently, this strategy has been used by teams not necessarily in a position of advantage.

Gotham Girls All-Stars take a knee to get the jam started faster at the WFTDA Championships 2011.

## Communication

Communication is essential in roller derby as different strategies can only be executed if any of the players on your team understand where they need to be. If a team are communicating well with each other, whether verbally or non-verbally, they should be telling each other where both jammers are on the track, where they need to be and what they are going to do next so that they can play effectively together as a team.

## Holding the inside line

This is a really fundamental part of strategy for playing roller derby. It sounds so simple but can be the difference between winning and losing a game.

Common sense tells us that taking the inside line is the shortest distance around the track so this is always the ideal route for a jammer to take. By making sure there is at least one blocker covering this area at all times, this route becomes unavailable, therefore impeding the jammer's progress in getting round the track.

## Passing the star

A jammer can give her helmet cover to her team's pivot so she can take over as the jammer for that team at any point during a jam. This is also known as 'passing the star'. Most commonly you will see a jammer doing this if she is injured or if her pivot is in a better position to score points than she is.

Team USA (red) hold the inside line to prevent Atomatrix jamming for Team USA (white) from getting through the pack on the inside.

## Walls

A wall is a form of blocking where two or more skaters work together to take up as much room on the track as possible in order to impede, slow down or trap the opposing jammer and prevent her from getting through the pack and scoring points. They can also be used to impede the movements of the blockers on the opposing team. Walls can be made using different formations depending on the situation on the track.

## Basic walls

The most basic of walls consists of two skaters, working together to cover the track laterally and prevent the opposing jammer from passing them. Two blockers can cover at least half the track if they stay close together while maintaining a wide stance. They will work together to cover the inside and outside areas of the track and communicate with each other to move laterally together with the jammer and prevent her from passing them.

This type of wall is typically formed starting from the inside line of the track and spreading out as far across the track as possible while the two skaters are still in close proximity to each other. A jammer will take every opportunity to leap through the tiniest of spaces so it is important that the blockers forming the wall don't leave any space for the jammer to sneak through. A strong and effective wall has the potential to prevent the opposing jammer from getting through the pack at all.

### Two x two

This is typically a defensive formation where the four blockers of one team in the pack can form two basic defensive walls. The position of the two walls can be different in different situations but is often one wall at the front and one at the back of the pack in order to cover as much ground as possible. Some teams like to keep their two walls close together to try to separate the opposing team's players from each other. These two walls will have to adapt to the situation on the track, and sometimes, at least one blocker will need to switch to playing offence at some point during the jam.

Oly Rollers Cosa Nostra Donnas make a basic two-wall in front of Gotham's jammer Bonnie Thunders at the WFTDA Championships 2011.

## Three-person dynamic walls

There are several different types of walls that can be made using three blockers. Using three blockers as opposed to two means that a larger area of the track is covered and that the wall can be more dynamic. With all of the following walls, if one blocker leaves the wall to hit the jammer out of bounds, the remaining two blockers can reposition themselves so that they are covering as much of the track as possible and there is always an effective wall in place.

## The web

This is a three-person wall where all three blockers skate side by side on the track and are touching each other at all times. As the jammer approaches the blockers in the wall, the wall will move according to the jammer's position on the track and prevent her from passing. The middle and external blockers on the side of the track where the jammer is positioned can contain the jammer while the third blocker can remain in place to keep the rest of the track covered or hit the jammer out of bounds if necessary to prevent her from moving forward.

Minnesota RollerGirls make a web three-wall in front of the Texas Rollergirls Texecutioners at the WFTDA Championships 2011.

Texas Rollergirls' Texecutioners make a web three-wall at the front of the pack at the WFTDA Championships 2011.

### Two in front

This is a three-person wall where there is a basic wall of two blockers skating in front of a third blocker who skates close behind them and uses them as an anchor for blocking an approaching jammer. The blocker at the back can knock the jammer out of bounds while the two-wall in front can keep the track covered. If the jammer manages to pass the blocker at the back, then the two person wall in the front will be able to hold her back. It's a double-layer of defence.

### One in front

This wall is just the same as the above but with a single blocker acting as an anchor in the front for a two-person wall behind. This can also be done with the person in front skating backwards so that she can see the position of all the skaters on the track more clearly and push and position her team-mates into the most effective place to block the opposing jammer as she approaches.

Team England's Metallikat and Juicy Lucy anchor off Frightning Bolt in three-wall with Frightning Bolt at the front at the Roller Derby World Cup 2011.

## Four-person walls
### The spoke

This is a heavily defensive wall where all four blockers are spread out across the track in a horizontal line, covering the width of the track in its entirety. This wall is often used when the opposing jammer is approaching the pack in a power jam situation when the opposing team has the advantage.

### The diamond

This is a technique using four blockers to form a diamond shape in the pack to make it more difficult for the opposing jammer to get through the pack and score points.

All four of Team Australia's blockers spread out across the track at the Roller Derby World Cup 2011.

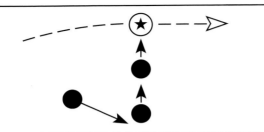

## Waterfalling or recycling

Waterfalling, also known as recycling, is a variation on the basic principle of walls that allows one of the blockers that make up the wall to leave the close proximity of the wall and engage the opposing jammer without sacrificing the dominance or position of the wall on the track. It can also be used to maintain the presence of a wall when one of the blockers who makes up the wall is picked off by an opposing blocker attempting to shut down the wall. This is achieved by the blockers in the wall rotating their positions so that the wall remains intact. When one skater leaves the wall, the other blocker rotates to take up her position and then another blocker from the same team will fill any gap that has arisen due to the rotation of the blockers in the wall. It means that if any member of the wall is taken away from her position, a team-mate will have that space covered at all times.

## Timing of walls

In order for walls to be effective, they must be made strategically, at the moment when it is necessary to block the opposing jammer or blockers. While blockers often skate together most of the time, and it is almost always beneficial to be working in close proximity with your team-mates, forming a wall is vital when the opposing jammer reaches the back of the pack. Making a wall in front of your own jammer as she is trying to get through the pack would not be the most effective thing to do, for instance. Making walls too early can also allow the opposing blockers the opportunity to break up those walls before they are really needed. When both jammers are in the pack, the use of walls becomes more complicated and has to be assessed carefully according to the situation at the given time.

Minnesota RollerGirls' blockers wall up in front of Olivia Shootin' John jamming for Teaxas Rollergirls Texecutioners at the WFTDA Championships 2011.

## Breaking walls

We have looked at forming defensive walls but how do you break up those walls in order to help your jammer get through? When you are devoted to playing offence, breaking up any walls formed by the opposing team is a vital part of your job as an offensive blocker. There are several ways that this can be done. One is to get in front of the wall and deliberately slow down in order to force the wall to split and go around you. Another way to shut down a wall is by hemming the opposing blockers in with your own blockers or to try to push the wall over to one side of the track so that your jammer can still pass through.

Gotham's blocker moves in from the inside to break up a wall of Rocky Mountain as Gotham's jammer Suzy Hotrod hits tha back of the pack at the WFTDA Championships 2011.

# PITCHIT DAVIS: *TALKING TO A STRATEGY COACH*

### What are the current trends in strategy for roller derby?

The trend is that we're starting to see strategy now. We've seen a lot of skating around and a lot of hitting but there was really no strategy involved to get to an end goal.

### How has strategy changed during the current roller derby revival?

New skaters coming into the sport are more and more likely to be athletes who are used to using strategy and understanding the bigger picture. They have to have an end goal. What is the end goal? Winning the game. How do we get there? Well, they draw themselves a roadmap and they say these are the things we need to do to win this game and so they start tearing it apart just like any good sport strategist would do, figuring out exactly what it would take to win a game no matter what the other team do and try to process it.

### What advice would you give to new skaters to learn effective strategy?

If you're a new skater with a new league and all they're doing is teaching you skate skills, you may want to ask 'when are we going to start learning strategy?' because strategy can be taught and learned before you're good at skating. Actually, strategy can be taught and learned by someone who doesn't skate at all so it is in your best interests as a new skater to start learning strategy right away.

### What advice would you give to more experienced skaters to play with effective strategy?

An experienced skater should know a little bit about strategy. If you are playing with a group that has an effective strategy, then you need to be learning it from that group, if you are playing against teams who have an effective strategy, you need to pay attention to what they're doing and see what works for them. You can do the same with video; you can watch games where effective strategy is happening and you can learn a lot from it.

### How did you learn strategy?

We decided that we needed to be able tell the new guys something that would help us win games and help them be effective quickly. So we developed a Default Strategy and we committed ourselves to it and worked it as much as we could so we were excellent at it and our new guys could feel confident that they knew what they were doing at all times.

### Can you describe the Default Strategy?

It is a basic strategy you can teach to anybody that is a good starting point for building a more complex strategy. If everybody knows what to default to in an emergency or in a situation where you don't know what to do, everybody will have an awareness of what is happening on the track at all times. We've all been there: you're in the middle of a game, and you're not really sure what to do. It doesn't seem smart to hit somebody right now because it's not going to help us win this game but on the other hand I don't know what to do, I'm just skating around. Default Strategy eliminates all of that. We wanted to know at every single second during game play what we should be doing and what we could expect the rest of our team to be doing in order to win this game.

### What other principles of strategy are you working on at the moment?

I'm trying to put together the next level to teach that to some of the leagues to whom I've already taught Default Strategy. A lot of them are figuring it out on their own but a lot of them want some input.

## What do you think the future holds for roller derby as a sport?

I think that it has a lot of opportunity. Will people ever be paid to play roller derby? I really have no idea. I think that would be interesting and maybe kinda cool. Roller derby could be big on TV again but it's going to take the right kind of marketing to make it happen. I think the most success will be in recreational roller derby. The things that will come above and below it are already starting, for instance, people trying to make a profession out of roller derby. People who get paid to play or tournament organisers who are trying to make it so that at least the roller derby player doesn't have to be out of pocket. And then we also have roller derby that's at levels below what the WFTDA does and is way more casual. It's just a case of show up and play when you want, pay when you show up and play when you can. I think all of it is going to expand but the one with the most success is going to be the WFTDA club type roller derby.

## How will strategy change over the next few years as roller derby develops?

I really have no idea. I would guess that like with anything, it would get to a point where the rules are pretty soundproof, pretty tight and they are going to have to nitpick the rules to find ways of beating other teams. I think that you will see a better rule set and you will see it become much more difficult to use them to your advantage to win. I also see, potentially, at the higher level, a pro roller derby if you will, with people who are paid to play roller derby. I think that rule set would be more relaxed and easier to play in and you wouldn't have to manipulate the rules so much to win games. It's hard to say what the future holds but there's potential for it to get a whole lot better, that's for sure.

# Fitness

# FIT FOR ROLLER DERBY?

Roller derby is a physically demanding, fast-paced contact sport that requires athletes to build high levels of cardiovascular fitness, strength, endurance, speed, agility, coordination and balance in order to play competitively. For people who are new to the sport, it is essential to spend some time building up all-round fitness in order to improve performance, and safety, on the track.

There are not only many health and fitness benefits for those who play roller derby on a regular basis, it is also an extremely enjoyable team sport. Playing roller derby is an excellent way to get fit and stay in shape. It works all of the major muscle groups and playing the sport regularly will tone and build muscle throughout the body, as well as building cardiovascular fitness and endurance.

Playing roller derby provides an excellent aerobic workout, strengthening the heart and lungs and making the body operate more efficiently.

Because of the physically demanding nature of roller derby, the body burns a lot of calories while playing, making it a great sport for athletes intending to lose weight. Roller skating burns up to 600 calories per hour so playing roller derby can burn even more than this due to the speed and intensity of the sport.

## Fitness benefits of playing roller derby

- Roller derby can improve cardiovascular fitness as well as muscle endurance and strength.
- It works all the muscle groups in the body.
- Playing roller derby burns a lot of calories.
- It improves balance, coordination and proprioception.
- Playing roller derby is a fun way to exercise without having to go to the gym.
- It is a team sport so is a great way to socialise and meet new people while getting fit at the same time.
- Playing a contact sport such as roller derby is a great way to beat the stress that can build up in day-to-day life.

# SKATER PROFILE: *HYPER LYNX, GOTHAM GIRLS' ROLLER DERBY, USA*

**How long have you been playing roller derby?**
Six and a half years.

**Did you skate before you played roller derby?**
The most skating I did growing up was on a family trip to Disneyworld. I skated for hours over a three-day period. I then found out about the Central Park Dance Skate Circle and started to learn how to rollerblade properly, about three months before discovering and joining derby.

**Did you play any other sports before you started playing roller derby?**
I did judo in junior high, tae kwon do in college and shaolin kung fu after moving to New York, for about two years each. Derby is the first sport I've kept at for more than two years …

**How has playing roller derby affected your overall health and fitness?**
It's the first sport that has motivated me to become a better athlete. Nothing makes me want to stay in shape and improve my fitness every year like wanting to keep competing at the highest level of the sport.

**How often do you practise on skates?**
During the season three to five times a week. In the off season, I try to go at least once a week.

**What other off-skates training do you do?**
I try to go to Muay Thai classes twice a week with Pilates beforehand. Every month or so I try to do anti-gravity yoga, to stretch my back! I used to do hot yoga once a week.

**Which other sports support roller derby?**
Speed and artistic skating, roller and ice hockey and soccer are good, along with martial arts and dance. Any sport with a lot of movement, coordination, body awareness and endurance supports roller derby.

**What training has helped you to improve most as a skater?**
Speed skating with plyometric land drills for strengthening, hockey drills for control and scrimmaging as often as possible. The dynamics on the track are so chaotic that you have to keep doing it to get better.

**What advice would you give new skaters about training for roller derby?**
Skate as often as you can. Get a set of outdoor wheels and go to the park. Find out about speed skating classes and dance skate parties in your area. Better yet, sign up for Gotham Girl Roller Derby's recreational league where our skaters will teach you how to skate and play derby at our practice facility (with a real derby track). General fitness and core strength go a long way, just like in any sport. The better shape you're in the better a derby player you will be.

**Do you have any other advice?**
Listen to your body, keep your equipment in check, and stay hydrated. Being able to keep on doing derby is as important as playing derby. The older you get the more maintenance your body needs; recovery is key, as well as flexibility and cross-training. Since we only skate in one direction, there are a lot of rotated hip injuries and body imbalances. Doing other activities that move your body in every direction and realigns it is very important. Realising that you're more fit than a lot of other people just by doing derby feels awesome. You're doing something fun and enjoyable, and you're getting fit in the process.

# SKATER PROFILE *MISS AMERICAN THIGHS, GOTHAM GIRLS ROLLER DERBY, USA*

**How long have you been playing roller derby?**
2012 will be my fifth season.

**Did you skate before you started roller derby?**
As a kid in the 1970s at the sunset roller rink in Iowa.

**Did you play any other sports before you started roller derby?**
Softball, basketball, track – pretty much from the time I was in kindergarten; volleyball from when I was a freshman in high school. When I moved to Brooklyn, I played softball with the local beer league which was fun, but not that healthy as many people played with a beer and or cigarette in their hand.

**How has playing roller derby affected your overall health and fitness?**
After high school, I would occasionally run around the block or try to walk as much as I could, but I basically gave up thinking of myself as an athlete. Derby became an activity that I enjoyed not only because the exercise made me feel better, but the support and camaraderie with the other skaters has encouraged me to keep with it. As a part of a team, I feel expected to be at my best.

**How often do you practise on skates?**
I aim for at least three times a week (around six hours).

**What additional off-skates training do you do and how often?**
I just discovered Barry's Bootcamp. I force myself to go to a gym to lift weights in the off season so I can remain competitive.

**Which other sports support playing roller derby?**
Any sport that builds strong lower body muscles, like volleyball or basketball.

**What training has helped you to improve the most as a skater?**
Aside from practise, practise, practise on the track? Strengthening my quads and hamstrings with weight training has made me more comfortable staying low on the track, lowering my centre of gravity, which in turn makes me more stable and my hits more powerful.

**Is there anything else you would like to share?**
The first time I tried out, I came straight from my job wearing my work clothes and rentals from Empire Skate, and borrowed pads from the skaters. After I left, I was completely charged and excited and thought I would die if I didn't get into the league. The women who started Gotham and nursed it through the first few years were supportive, friendly, fun and made me want to be a part of the community. I didn't make it the first year, but it drove me to train for the next season's try-outs. When I finally made it, I jumped up and down like I won a car on The Price is Right!

# WHAT IS FITNESS?

The word 'fitness' is an umbrella term that is used to cover all of the different physical attributes required for exercise. This includes a more general state of overall health and well-being, as well as skills that relate to a specific sport or sports. The attributes included in physical fitness can be separated into attributes that relate to the overall physical health of an athlete, and attributes that relate to an athlete's level of skill.

This chapter looks at how the different aspects of physical fitness play a part in roller derby and how to train for each aspect of physical fitness involved in playing the sport.

### Cardiovascular fitness or aerobic fitness

This refers to the efficient working of the heart, the lungs and the circulatory system in order to supply oxygen to the muscles during physical activity. When you exercise regularly, you can increase the efficiency of your heart and lungs, enabling more blood and oxygen to be pumped around the body. As the body becomes fitter, it becomes more efficient at supplying blood and oxygen to the working muscles, and the muscles become more efficient at using oxygen to make fuel for exercise.

There are many health benefits related to cardiovascular fitness. It can improve the condition of the heart and lungs, as well as reducing the risk of heart disease, lung cancer, type two diabetes, stroke and many other diseases.

A good level of cardiovascular fitness is definitely beneficial for playing roller derby. The stronger and more efficient your heart and lungs are, the easier it will be to skate faster, recover quicker and keep going for longer.

Any type of aerobic exercise will provide effective cardiovascular fitness training. Swimming, running or rowing are common examples but any exercise that significantly raises your heart rate and keeps it raised can be considered as cardiovascular exercise.

Cardiovascular fitness increases the efficiency of the heart and lungs. Rowing is one of many different types of cardiovascular exercise.

## Muscular endurance

This refers to the ability of a muscle or muscle group to repeat and sustain a particular movement or series of movements for an extended period of time. Muscular endurance is determined by how well your slow twitch muscle fibres are developed.

In the body, there are two main types of muscle fibres: fast twitch and slow twitch. Fast twitch muscle fibres can exert a great amount of force for a very limited amount of time, and slow twitch muscle fibres cannot exert as much force but can sustain effort for a much longer period of time.

Muscular endurance is important for roller derby and, in fact, any other sport that requires athletes to perform for longer periods of time. It is muscular endurance that will enable you to keep skating at your best through the duration of a bout without feeling fatigued.

Any cardiovascular activity such as running, cycling or especially skating longer distances will help to increase the muscular endurance needed for playing roller derby.

Muscular endurance is the ability to sustain a movement or series of movements for an extended period of time. Long-distance running is a good way of training for endurance.

## Muscular strength

This refers to how much force your muscles can exert in a single effort or movement. Muscular strength is different from muscular endurance. Muscular strength refers to how much force your muscles can exert and is controlled by your fast twitch muscle fibres which are used when you require quick bursts of energy.

Muscular strength is important in roller derby because this is where you get the push from your muscles required in order to leap, jump and propel yourself forward and ensure that your movements are powerful.

Any kind of resistance training or plyometric exercises are effective types of training for muscular strength. Strength training also increases fuel-storage capacity in the muscles, enabling your muscles to work for longer without refuelling and delaying the onset of muscle fatigue.

Resistance exercises such as push-ups can be used to increase muscular strength.

## Speed

Speed refers to how fast you can perform a movement or series of movements. Speed is important in roller derby, especially when jamming. Speed skating is the best way to train to skate at high speed.

Speed skating is a great way to train to learn the best technique for skating at high speed. Speed is important for roller derby – especially when jamming.

## Power

Power is the combination of strength and speed together. It is the ability of a muscle to maximally contract in an instant to create explosive movement. An example of this is the momentum you gather when skating at speed and then jumping: the faster you are travelling and the stronger you are, the more explosive and powerful your jump will be. Plyometric exercises are an excellent training for executing powerful movements.

## Agility

Agility refers to the ability to change the position of the body quickly and effectively, usually involving a rapid whole-body movement and change of direction. It involves a combination of balance, coordination, speed, strength, endurance and stamina.

Agility is important in roller derby in order to be able to move around the track, change position rapidly and respond quickly to the constantly changing situation. It is important for all positions but particularly for jammers who need to juke and dodge blockers effectively. It is also important for defensive blockers who need to be able to move with the jammer and get in her way.

The best way to train to increase agility for playing roller derby is on skates. Practising changing position on the track, stopping and starting, spinning, jumping and changing direction will increase your ability to change position rapidly whenever necessary.

## Balance

Balance is the ability to maintain the body's stability while going through a range of motions. In order to do so, your head, chest and hips should all be positioned over your feet. Balancing requires input from a number of senses through the brain, as well as the motor system simultaneously controlling the

Agility is the ability to change the position of the body quickly and effectively. Agility will help any roller derby skater to respond quickly to the rapidly changing situation on the track.

Balance is the ability to maintain the body's stability while going through a range of motions. Practising different movements on skates will help you to increase your ability to balance.

muscle actions. The senses must detect changes of body position, and the muscles must respond accordingly through the brain to maintain stability. Balance is a dynamic process that applies to all the movements the body makes. Whether walking, skating or running, the body is continuously losing and regaining balance.

Balance is a vital aspect of any type of skating because moving around on wheels means it is much more difficult to sustain balance than when travelling on a stable surface. It is balance that will allow you to remain stable when getting knocked or hit, or land that perfect apex jump.

Spending as much time on skates as possible will inevitably help to increase your ability to balance; the more comfortable you are on eight wheels, the more likely you will be able to balance effectively. There are other things you can do to improve your balance effectively. Doing yoga is fantastic training for this, using a balance board or practising standing, hopping or skating on one leg and then the other, as well as any other set of moves that challenge your balance. Good core strength will also enable you to more easily achieve good balance and remain stable when your balance is challenged.

## Flexibility

Flexibility is determined by how far a muscle can stretch its fibres. When a muscle contracts, its fibres shorten, and when a muscle expands, its fibres lengthen. The further the muscle fibres can stretch and lengthen, the longer an eccentric movement it can make. The more the muscles fibres can stretch, the more flexible the muscle becomes.

Flexibility is a very important aspect of overall physical fitness. Maintaining a high level of flexibility will reduce the risk of injury and improve your performance in any sport.

The best way to increase flexibility is to stretch. Stretching every muscle group regularly will increase flexibility and help to keep muscles and joints supple. Stretching before and especially after exercise is also important but make sure your body is warmed up before stretching, otherwise you will risk overstretching your muscles which can lead to strains or pulls.

## Proprioception

Proprioception is the ability of the body to be aware of the orientation of its limbs in space. It is distinct from balance, which is the ability of the body to stay stable. Proprioception is what enables us to carry out movements with our limbs without looking at exactly where they are, for example driving while looking at the road, or skating forwards while looking behind you.

Proprioception is important for roller derby because when playing roller derby, the body and mind have to do so many things at the same time. Your body needs to be able to skate and move around on the track while your eyes are watching out for what is happening and where your team-mates, and the members of the opposing team, are on the track. There just isn't time for you to be able to look at what your feet are doing in a game. Having good proprioception will allow you to feel confident that you know where your limbs are and where to put them while remaining focused on the game.

Practising yoga, the Alexander Technique, juggling, slacklining and doing exercises on a balance board and any other movements that challenge spatial awareness and reaction time are all effective ways to improve proprioception.

Doing exercises on a balance board is a great way to increase proprioception.

# WHICH MUSCLES ARE USED IN PLAYING ROLLER DERBY?

Roller skating primarily uses the muscles that flex and extend the hip, knee and ankle joints. These include the quadriceps, hamstrings and gluteal muscles and also the hip abductors and adductors which move the leg away from and towards the midline of the body. The bent-over stance known as 'derby position' also uses all the core muscles including the muscles in the lower back.

The muscles that begin at the hips enable your legs to push, giving you forward momentum. The gluteal muscles tighten as the quadriceps help your knees to push off the ground, propelling you forwards on your skates. The hamstrings also form part of this push. The side-to-side movement is very important in roller derby, especially in lateral skating and crossovers, so it important to be able to shift body weight easily while remaining in balance and be able to twist from the waist to change direction using the abdominal muscles and obliques.

The muscles in the lower body have to support the entire body weight while balancing and moving on eight wheels. The core muscles provide the body with the stability it needs to skate around the track, as well as to hit and take hits without falling. The core is made up of the abdominal, lower back and muscles at the sides of the torso, as well as the gluteal muscles, quadriceps and hamstrings.

The upper body is also used in playing roller derby in order to balance and support the lower body, as well as when using contact. Legal contact areas such as the shoulders are used for hitting, and all the muscles in the back, shoulders and upper body are used for blocking, counter-blocking and changing direction. These include the deltoids, trapezius, rhomboids, latissimus dorsi, the muscles in the rotator cuff and the biceps and triceps in the arms. The forearms are often used for giving or taking assists with your own team, as well as anchoring when blocking and making contact with your team-

mates when forming defensive walls, but pushing, pulling or grabbing members of the opposing team is against the rules.

## Main muscles used in playing roller derby

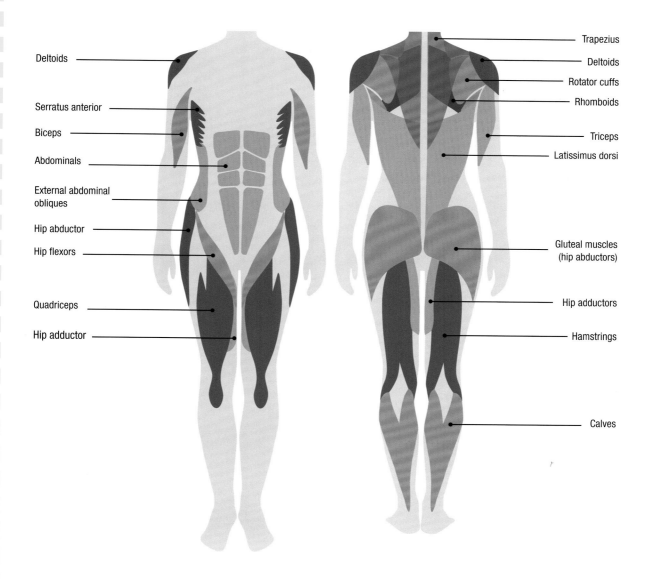

Deltoids

Serratus anterior

Biceps

Abdominals

External abdominal obliques

Hip abductor

Hip flexors

Quadriceps

Hip adductor

Trapezius

Deltoids

Rotator cuffs

Rhomboids

Triceps

Latissimus dorsi

Gluteal muscles (hip abductors)

Hip adductors

Hamstrings

Calves

## Derby position

Derby position is the optimum position a skater should adopt for playing roller derby. It is often compared to sitting in a chair or a bar stool. The body should be in a squatting position with the bottom low, feet shoulder width apart, knees bent and almost parallel to the ground with the centre of gravity directly over the ankles, the back should be angled but relatively straight, not hunched over the knees and with the arms and elbows close in.

This position allows the skater maximum stability while also allowing her to build up speed and power when doing crossovers. If you are in derby position, it is harder to fall and if you do fall, you'll fall on your knees, which is a lot safer than falling backwards because your knees are protected by kneepads as part of the safety regulations. Proper derby stance or derby position will also enable you to positionally block effectively as well as being a good base for hitting. It will allow you to move quickly and nimbly on your feet without losing balance. This position will vary from person to person because all skaters have their own individual style and physique. However, this is the basic principle for an effective position for playing roller derby.

Derby position is similar to ready position, which is used in many sports such as boxing and tennis, and is the position from which the body can react and change position most quickly. In derby position with the feet shoulder-width apart, the bottom low, the knees bent and the weight centred over the ankles, you are ready to move in any direction and react quickly. The right angles at every joint mean the body is the more stable, and will prevent injuries from occurring.

# SKATER PROFILE *LULU DEMON, TERMINAL CITY ROLLERGIRLS, VANCOUVER, CANADA.*

**How long have you been playing roller derby?**
Since August 2006.

**Did you skate before you started roller derby?**
One of my strongest childhood memories is of the Fisher Price blue and yellow adjustable skates I got for my birthday. But growing up in England I spent my youth rollerblading around Hyde Park and dodging taxis on Kensington High Street.

**Did you play any other sports before you started roller derby?**
Roller blading was my passion from the age of 11. Most evenings I could be found playing street hockey or trying out new tricks on the cones outside the Albert Hall. I prided myself on being the only girl who played street hockey: they called me 'Mad Dog Lucy'. I learnt to snowboard aged 19 and one of the reasons I moved to Canada was to be closer to the mountains. Not that I have much time these days to do anything other than derby.

**How has roller derby affected your overall health and fitness?**
It has had a huge impact. I have always been an active person. But it has given me a focus for my fitness, and I have learnt so much about nutrition, workout plans and maximising certain muscle groups. Plus I just love going to practice so it makes being fit much easier than slogging it out in a gym.

**How often do you practise on skates?**
Three to four times a week: three-hour practice sessions plus dryland.

**What additional off-skates training do you do and how often?**
We often add dryland conditioning onto our practices. Once a week we do plyometrics. Before our Saturday practices we do an all-over body conditioning and warm-up in the changing rooms of the roller rink. I have also been doing some of the Insanity workouts: 20 minute of high intensity interval training that kick my ass like nothing else. I am working out or skating four to six times per week on average when I am in training mode.

**Which other sports support roller derby?**
The obvious ones are speed skating and hockey. We also have marathon runners, basketball players, competitive road racers, professional snowboarders and they all kick ass.

**What type of training has helped you to improve the most as a skater?**
In the last year the off-skates training that I have been doing has made a huge difference to my performance. Plyometrics and cross-training have given me more core strength and explosive power. I have also been working closely with speed skaters to work on my form and stride efficiency and I feel like I am finally getting faster with less effort! I am also a training camp junkie: when I am not coaching at them I am soaking up as much derby knowledge and new skills as possible.

### What advice do you have for new skaters about training for roller derby?

Don't think that just because you spend X number of hours on skates that you are fit. When we skate we only use certain muscles groups and while you do need to spend time building these up, don't forget the rest of your body.

Cross-training and core strength are key to preventing injuries and maximising performance. The reason we have so many knee injuries is because we don't work on the stabiliser muscles in our knees and our groins. Start doing dryland training together as a league and you'll see injuries go down and performance go up.

# TRAINING FOR ROLLER DERBY

In order to play roller derby well we need to ensure that as well as having a passion for the sport, a good understanding or the rules and strategy, great motivation and team spirit, our bodies are in top physical condition. As well as cardiovascular fitness, agility, endurance, speed and strength it is also essential that our bodies can exert maximum energy for short periods and then recover quickly.

Each jam only lasts a maximum of two minutes, with only 30 seconds in between jams so ideally, your body needs to be able to recover and be ready to go all out again with only 30 seconds rest. In order to play roller derby to the best of our ability, we can train specifically to meet the physical demands that the sport places on us as athletes.

## Training on skates
### Training movement patterns
Part of any sport-specific training involves training the body to perform series of movement patterns. In addition to training the body and the muscles to cope, it is also important to execute these movement patterns so that the body develops muscle memory for these specific series. This will enable the body to perform them more quickly, more powerfully and endure them for longer. Acceleration, deceleration, stopping, crossovers, duck runs, toe-stop running, stepping, spinning, jumping, hitting, skating laterally, falling and recovering can all be broken down into separate movements and practising all of these movements until you can do them comfortably will undoubtedly improve your performance.

# ON-SKATES TRAINING WITH KAMIKAZE KITTEN: JUMPS

I like jumping. Jumping is fun. Jumping is like flying just for a very short period of time. I'm going to go through the basics of several jumps and how they are useful for roller derby.

Remember to practise with all your protective gear on, not just for your own safety, but for your confidence too. That includes elbow pads – I've still got a ridiculous scar from the time I had everything else on except my elbow pads and decided to jump Lola Vulcano on a quiet New Jersey road.

## Vertical jump

This is a really useful jump for clearing the limbs of downed skaters and sudden obstacles. It's simple to learn because you just, well, jump. It's worth practising at different speeds so that you are confident with jumping on the track when you don't have the added height and distance provided by a speedy approach.

Start off by jumping over a line or mark on the ground so that there is no chance of catching your skates and faceplanting.

1 Approach your mark with a moderate speed.

2 Compress your legs to give your quadriceps power.

3 Jump!

4 Land and immediately compress your legs to absorb the power and protect your knees.

❶　　　　❷　　　　❸　　　　　　　❹

You can see from the front how your knees stay together; use your arms for mid-air balance and you will often naturally leave a gap between your feet and where the very highest point of the object that you are jumping is located.

*A lot of skaters prefer to do a tuck jump. This is a jump whereby you simply pull your knees up to your chest from an upright position. This movement is what provides you with your object clearance, but I find that it sends too much shock up to my knees on the landing as it seems harder to me to have a bended knee landing. I also tend to overbalance backwards as my weight is too far behind my skates on the landing.

## Leap

Whereas the vertical jump is for height, the leap is for distance. This jump is the easiest to learn because it can be done with very little time in the air to start off with. All you are doing is hopping from one foot to the other. If you want to get more power and distance into the jump there are a few things you can do.

This jump is most commonly used for jumping the apex. The biggest mistake when planning your apex jump is thinking that you can turn a curve while in the air. Always plan your approach so that the last stride or so of your approach, your launch spot and your landing spot are in a straight line.

**1**    **2**    **3**    **4**

1 Skate faster on the approach – the faster you are skating, the greater the distance you will cover during the 'in air' portion of the jump.

2 Launch off your front axle and toe stop. In order to transfer the power from your compressed leg you need something stable and solid to launch from.

3 Leap!

4 Land on your outside foot and compress this foot to absorb the power.

An alternative option from launching off your toe stop is to twist your foot so that it is at an angle, therefore your wheels are providing the friction to allow you to launch.

## Lateral leap

This time you want to cover as much distance across the track as possible. The more of the track you can cover in one jump, the better chance you have of taking advantage of gaps that appear in walls and the better you will get at juking blockers.

The key to a good lateral leap is the compression in your power leg. By dropping your shoulder in the opposite direction to the one that you are about to leap in, you can increase the amount of momentum and cover a greater distance too. So let's go through the process of jumping from the inside of the track to the outside of the track.

1 Moments before you leap, put all of your weight down onto your inside leg while at the same time dropping your shoulder towards your inside knee.

2 Powerfully straighten your inside leg whilst throwing your shoulders towards the outside of the track. Most of the power will come from your inside leg heel, your foot will be in a similar position to when you plough. As you launch off the ground, get the final extra push off the toe stop of the inside foot.

3 Leap!

4 Land on your outside foot and compress this foot to absorb the power but also allowing your body weight to reach the outside of the track.

The next step, once you've nailed this jump in one direction, is to work on the return jump. Practise with trainers on first, until you can convert the landing compression power into a return spring in the opposite direction.

## Same leg hop

This isn't a particularly flashy or big jump, but it can be really useful for getting you out of a tight spot or getting over a sudden small obstacle. Most of the power for this hop comes from the energy of going from a flat-footed position to a pointed toe position so it can be done without much build-up at all.

With very little set up for this jump it's much more about balance and being comfortable hopping and landing on one leg. The advantage of a same leg hop comes from being able to hang most of your body over the inside or outside line without touching out of bounds. Alternatively, you can hop over a foot that is covering the inside line and keep your body tucked out of the way. Because it doesn't take any wind up and is a very fast jump to execute this move often takes blockers by surprise.

1 As you approach, put all of your weight onto your outside leg.

2 Compress your outside leg to launch off the ground.

3 Hop!

4 Compress your leg as you land on the same leg.

5 Continue skating.

# TURNS AND SPINS

Turns and spins can be split into four categories.

1 Stepping direction changes where you lift one foot at a time.
2 Jumping direction changes where there is a moment of having no feet on the ground.
3 Swooping direction changes, where you apply pressure to one edge of your skate and keep that pressure until you have turned all the way around (similar to a car driving around a hairpin bend).
4 Axle rotations, where you lift either your front or your rear wheels in order to pivot on one axle.

The trick to turning around when moving is to keep your wheels parallel with the direction that you are travelling. If you consistently fall when trying to turn around by stepping or jumping, check out your feet first. Are you planting them accurately so that there is zero friction being applied by your wheels?

## 180 degree step

This is the first turn that I ever learned. Back then we used to call it 'open the door, close the door' and it involves a stepping direction change.

1 Skating forwards, lift your right leg so that you briefly glide on just your left leg.

2 Turn your right foot 180° around whilst it is in the air.

3 Place your right foot on the ground when it hits the 180° mark and immediately remove your weight from your left foot. (You'll now be gliding backwards on one leg .)

4 Turn your left foot around 180° and place it on the ground.

Easy!

## 180 degree jump

Some skaters may prefer the jump around method of turning. Get comfortable with your two-footed jumps first. You don't need very much height, but you do want a little bit of time in the air so that you have enough time to complete the spin.

So now we'll add the turn.

1 Compress your knees a little before you jump.

2 Jump from heel to toe, so you launch off the ground from your front wheels rather than from a flat-footed position.

3 Spin your shoulders in the direction you want to go in! It is your upper body that is providing the direction change that will result in your feet turning around.

4 Stop turning as soon as you are facing the opposite direction.

5 Compress your knees slightly on landing.

You don't have to be too enthusiastic with spinning your body around or you may over-spin. A 180° spin is easy to achieve with very little time in the air. If you are struggling to land exactly, then pick a point that is 180° behind your starting point and look straight at it as soon as you leave the ground.

If you are struggling with balance on the landing then stagger your feet slightly to help prevent you from tipping forwards or backwards.

Once you've nailed it, you can start adding some more height just for fun. More compression in the take-off, and pulling your knees higher when in the air will give you extra height.

## Sidesurf turn

Have you been practising sidesurfing? That's skating with your feet pointing in opposite directions. When you first start out, you'll probably find that rather than skating in a straight line you end up going in a wide circle unless you are extremely flexible.

This is actually a useful skill in itself, especially when blocking skaters over the boundary lines. By making yourself very wide, you reduce the area that a skater who has been pushed out of bounds can return to the track. Similarly, by turning 180° you are in the perfect position to hop on your toe stops and track clockwise around the track – maximising the effectiveness of your hit.

1 With all of your weight on your front (left) foot, lift your heel axle of your right foot off the ground and rotate your right foot 180° on your front axle.

2 Rock your weight evenly over both feet, and apply pressure to the insides of both feet to turn.

3 When you have reached the desired direction, lift your weight off your heels so that you can spin your front axles so that your feet are parallel again.

**❶**          **❷**          **❸**

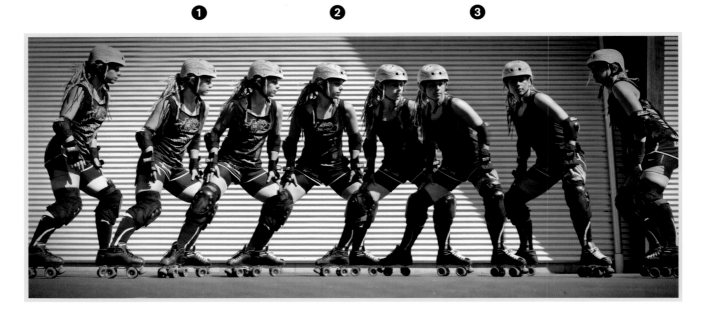

If you are concerned about receiving a hit to the chest when in this position then simply add an extra 90° to your turn. Making it a 270° instead of a 180° turn, completing it with your back to the track and your chest to the boundary.

## One-foot spin

One-foot spins are one of those skills that are useful to have just in case. You can't always choose when you get hit during scrimmage, and spinning in general is a brilliant way of turning momentum that is designed to move you around the track, into a direction change that keeps you in bounds. It just might happen that when you get hit, you only have one foot on the ground.

The basic way to do this spin is to jump around 180°. Everything is in balance when you land. Option two is to pivot on your axle. Technically you can pivot on either your front axle or your rear axle, but I prefer to pivot on my front axle as a lot of my direction changes come from the ball of my foot.

1 Skate on one foot while grinning like an idiot.

2 Raise the rear wheels of that foot off the ground.

3 Turn your shoulders 180° (your feet should follow).

4 Put your rear wheels back on the ground as soon as your foot is facing in the opposite direction.

5 If you overbalance once backwards just drop your other foot down in order to stabilise yourself.

## 360 degree jump

Jumping 360° isn't that hard. It's just a case of timing
your landing and getting enough air to complete 360°
of turning before you land back on the ground.

1 Compress your legs (more than for a 180° turn)
and at the same time, wind your body so that you
are facing the opposite direction to the one you will
be spinning with your shoulders. In this example I'm
spinning anticlockwise so I'll spin my upper body
clockwise 90° as my legs are bending.

2 As you straighten your legs quickly into the
jump, forcefully twist your upper body around in an
anticlockwise direction (the direction of the spin).

3 Jump!

4 Land with your legs staggered to help your
balance and neutralise some of the residual
spinning' force.

## Stomp and spin

Much like the original 180° step spin that we covered, the stomp and spin incorporates a hop from one foot to the other.

The key is to not have both of your feet on the ground simultaneously.

We call it the stomp and spin because the stomp element reminds you to place 100 per cent of your weight onto one foot and then spring around 180° in the air before landing on the other foot.

One of the key advantages to this spin is it has a very small footprint, making it a useful spin to use when passing through small gaps in walls (of blockers). Its advantage over sidesurfing your way through the wall is in what happens if you receive a block to the chest as you are passing between the blockers. You are already rotating in the direction you want to go in and any additional force in that direction (which is the only legal force) will just get you there faster. By landing on one foot that is facing 180° backwards, this force should also shoot you forwards and away from the wall. Snazzy!

1 Stomp (or put) all of your weight onto your right foot.

2 Jump off this foot and land on your right foot that is now pointing backwards.

3 Practise the move going through smaller and smaller gaps – the sideways position of your hips as you pass through the gap should help you squeeze through gaps that you couldn't get through with your hips facing forwards.

# TRAINING OFF-SKATES

You can train for speed, endurance, agility and strength on skates but many people don't have access to indoor or outdoor spaces that are appropriate for this type of training outside of their regular team or league practices. And although it goes without saying that the more time spent on skates the better for playing roller derby, some additional off-skates training can be very beneficial in terms of enabling you to focus on certain areas of fitness specific to this sport. All the most accomplished roller derby skaters I have ever spoken to highly recommend off-skates training to supplement their on-skates practice.

### Interval training

Interval training is something that has helped me a lot recently – especially with jamming. It is perfect for roller derby because it trains your body to perform at maximum capacity for short periods and then recover quickly. Interval training is a type of training that involves short periods of high-intensity exercise followed by periods of low-intensity exercise that are repeated during one training session. It can be done using most types of cardiovascular exercise but running, cycling and rowing are most common.

### How interval training works

Interval training uses both the aerobic and anaerobic systems as fuel for the body to exercise (see page 141). During the periods of high intensity, the anaerobic system uses glycogen stored in the muscles as fuel. The anaerobic system fuels your muscles without oxygen and produces lactic acid. In the periods of low intensity, the body breaks down the lactic acid that has built up.

It is thought that by performing high-intensity intervals that produce lactic acid during training, the body adapts and burns lactic acid more efficiently during exercise. This means athletes can exercise at a higher intensity for a longer period of time before fatigue or muscle pain slows them down.

### Interval training for roller derby

In roller derby, a bout is made up of two 30-minute periods. Each period is made up of a series of jams, which can last up to two minutes each, with a 30-second break in between. Ideally, we need to train so that the body is able to cope with the worst-case scenario under these circumstances. The worst-case scenario is that each jam will last the full two minutes and that skaters will be required to go on in consecutive jams. This means that skaters need to be able to exert themselves at maximum capacity for a full two minutes and recover in 30 seconds and keep this going for a period of 30 minutes before having a substantial break. In reality, this would rarely happen as jams often get called off before the full two minutes and skater line-ups are switched so that each skater gets enough time to rest between jams. It is possible to train for this using interval training.

### The benefits of interval training

Interval training helps to improve performance and increase speed and endurance by increasing the body's ability to deliver oxygen to the working muscles, which is also known as cardiovascular efficiency. It also produces an increased tolerance to the build-up of lactic acid. In addition, it helps athletes to increase the intensity of their training without overtraining and therefore helps avoid injuries caused by repetitive overuse. Many sources also claim that more calories are burned during periods of high intensity exercise as opposed to slow, endurance exercise. It is a great way of cross-training for many different sports, roller derby being only one of them.

An important thing to remember when doing interval training is that there needs to be a marked difference between the levels of exertion in the high intensity periods and the low intensity periods, for example walking or jogging slowly for low intensity and sprinting for high intensity. The recovery periods are just as important as the periods of high intensity.

## Interval training routines

Every person should work out their own individual interval training routine based on their level of fitness and what they want to achieve from their training. Designing the right training can be very sophisticated or quite casual. It is best for beginners to start with shorter periods of intensity and longer periods of rest and gradually build-up the level and duration of intensity, duration and frequency of training, and reduce the periods of rest to speed up recovery time.

### Safety tips for interval training

- Always warm up for at least 5 minutes before any interval training.
- You should be in good health and have a good level of basic aerobic fitness before performing any type of high-intensity training. Interval training is very demanding on the heart, lungs and muscles.
- Set yourself realistic goals based on your actual level of fitness.
- Start slowly with longer periods of rest between intervals of high intensity.
- Build up the intensity and duration slowly over an extended period of time.
- Always cool down and stretch after training.

# SKATER PROFILE *MOLOTOV M. PALE, TEXAS ROLLERGIRLS, USA*

**How long have you been playing roller derby?**
Five years

**Did you skate before playing roller derby?**
I probably hadn't been on roller skates since the third grade. I remember having to break down and learn the crossover. It took me about a year to learn how to skate well enough to feel comfortable bouting at full intensity and put on public games.

**Did you play any other sports before you started playing roller derby?**
I played a little of everything growing up: soccer, softball, basketball, but nothing very well. The first sport I felt really competent and competitive at was rugby. This was a serious indicator of my derby future – I was completely compelled both on the subcultural, fringe sport level and the full-contact, not-afraid-to-get-hurt intensity level.

**How has roller derby affected your overall health and fitness?**
Roller derby has had an incredibly positive influence on my fitness level and aspirations. Early on I made healthier lifestyle choices because I wanted to feel good and strong for practices and games. At the level I compete at now, I am continually inspired by the physical strength and stamina of the athletes I am surrounded by.

**How often do you practise on skates?**
I spend seven to ten hours a week in my skates.

**What additional off-skates training do you do and how often?**
My team warm up with a mixture of plyometrics, strength training and running for an hour. I run short distance (two to six miles) and do some strength training on my own. I love group classes like Pilates and spin classes. I want to take some kickboxing classes this off-season.

**Which other sports support roller derby?**
All kinds. Anything on skates (ice or roller). Hockey incorporates the skating agility and learning how to expertly leverage your body for powerful and effective blocks.

**What type of training has helped you to improve most as a skater?**
Probably just the sheer number of hours I've put in on my skates, sweating it out with all kinds of skaters. I've learned so much from an array of derby mentors. I think focusing on my overall fitness level through cross-training and running has been really great for me this past season. I think it's about balance – you can't overload on one focused area in my opinion. I've felt and performed the best when I've had a balance of nutrition, strength and conditioning that felt challenging but sustainable for me.

**What advice do you have for new skaters about training for roller derby?**
Stretching is so important. Nutrition and adequate sleep is huge for injury prevention. Also limiting the toxins in your body: if you're serious about derby it should have some real bearing on decisions you make regarding drugs and alcohol – everything you put in your body really. A lot of skaters get injured early on because their muscles aren't prepared. Easing into it with a recreational derby programme is a great option. Also just putting in some real hours at a gym before you throw yourself into the derby world so your body is better prepared.

# SKATER PROFILE: *DOUBLE CLUTCH, GOTHAM GIRLS ROLLER DERBY, USA*

**How long have you been playing roller derby?**
Three years; I'm beginning my fourth season with Gotham.

**Did you skate before playing roller derby?**
I skated on inline skates recreationally.

**Did you play any other sports before you started roller derby**
I was a competitive runner for more than 20 years, competing in hundreds of road races: I competed in three full marathons. After that, I segued into triathlons, competing in the sprint and Olympic-distance triathlons for six years and then I found derby.

**How has playing roller derby affected your overall health and fitness?**
Roller derby has changed my body. With each sport I do, my body adapts to that sport. I have very good endurance as a result of my marathon running and triathlon competitions and I have very good general strength as a result of my weight lifting.

**How often do you practise on skates?**
Three to five times a week depending on where we are in the season. These practices are made up of league, team and speed skating practices.

**What additional off-skates training do you do and how frequently?**
I supplement my skating with weight training and yoga.

**Which other sports do you think support playing roller derby?**
Hockey, soccer, basketball, rugby – any team sport; also running, triathlons and gymnastics.

**What type of training has helped you to improve most as a skater?**
Speed skating and going to league practices to learn strategy for derby.

**What advice would you give to new skaters about fitness for roller derby?**
They need to supplement their skating with off-skates training such as weight training. It's very important to keep your body strong. Also, I think doing cardio training is beneficial for skaters in helping to improve overall fitness. Yoga also helps to balance the intense training you receive as a derby skater, and getting enough rest is necessary too.

# CORE TRAINING

Core strength, also known as core stability, is a key area of fitness in training for roller derby. It supports the body for the contact aspect of the sport and is also essential for balancing and being steady on skates while moving at high speed. Core muscles are what enable our bodies to remain upright, control our movements and remain balanced, especially when on skates.

### Benefits of core training

Strong core muscles improve posture as they reduce the strain on the spine. Because the core muscles stabilise the spine from the neck and shoulders down to the pelvis, they are the source of all power to the limbs. Powerful movements from the arms and legs are generated from the centre of the body, not from the limbs in isolation, and these are crucial to skating, jumping, manoevring, blocking and taking hits. A strong core can also help to correct any imbalances in posture that can lead to injury.

### Defining the core

The core comprises all the muscles that align, move and stablilise the trunk of the body and maintain its upright position. This essentially means the abdominal muscles, the muscles in your back that support the length of the spine and the muscles in your sides. Some would also include the hip flexors, hamstring group, quadriceps and the gluteal muscles which support the pelvis. The core muscles are both the muscles that are on the surface as well as the deeper internal muscles.

### Building the core

To build a strong core, it is important to train a variety of muscles that span from below your hips to your shoulders. Many people think of the core only as the abdominal muscles but it is important to train all over to achieve the best results. Core exercises are most effective when they engage many muscles throughout the torso that cross several joints and work together to coordinate stability. Core muscles need to work as a unit, contracting at the same time across joints in order to stabilise the spine.

There are a huge range of core exercises, but it is up to the individual to discover what works best for them. I can only recommend a few in this book. Do your own research to find those that work best for what you want to achieve in your own training.

### Core muscles

- **Rectus abdominus:** located along the front of the abdomen, this is often referred to as the 'six-pack'.
- **Erector spinae:** this group of three muscles runs along your neck to your lower back.
- **Multifidus:** found under the erector spinae along the vertebral column, these extend and rotate the spine.
- **External obliques:** located on the side and front of the abdomen.
- **Internal obliques:** located under the external obliques, running in the opposite direction.
- **Transverse abdominus (TVA):** located under the obliques, it is the deepest of the abdominal muscles (muscles of your waist) and wraps around your spine for protection and stability.
- **Hip flexors:** located in front of the pelvis and upper thigh. They include the psoas major, iliacus, rectus femoris, pectineus, sartorius.
- **Gluteus medius and minimus:** at the side of the hip.
- **Gluteus maximus, hamstring group, piriformis:** located in the back of the hip and upper thigh.
- **Quadriceps:** located along the front of the thigh.

## Core exercises

### Front plank

Lie on your front on an exercise mat with your elbows beneath your shoulders, hands clasped together and forearms resting on the floor beneath your chest. Raise your body off the floor so that the only contact with the mat is made by your feet and your forearms. Your body should be in a flat, straight line. Pull in all your core muscles and hold the plank position for as long as your can before lowering yourself back to the floor. Repeat as many times as is required for your training session.

To make this exercise more challenging try lifting one leg off the ground for a few seconds before lowering the leg and repeating with the other leg.

### Side plank

This is a variation of the front plank position. Try moving from a front plank to a side plank on one side, over to a front plank and then to a side plank on the other side, holding each for a set amount of time.

Lie on your right side on an exercise mat, with your right arm under your right shoulder and your forearm and hand resting on the floor. Your legs should be straight and slightly parted, with your left leg over the top and in front of your right. Raise your right hip off the floor until your body makes a straight line, with your weight supported on your forearm and feet. Make sure your body is aligned: your hips should not be rotated and your bottom should be tucked in.

Stretch your left arm up to the ceiling or place your left hip if you prefer. Hold the position for as you can and then repeat on the other side.

### Bridge

The bridge is a great core exercise that works your gluteal muscles and hamstrings in particular. It will help to stabilise your pelvis and prevent injuries.

Lie on your back with your legs bent at the knee and your feet flat on the floor. Keeping your feet flat on the floor, slowly raise your bottom off the ground so that your weight is supported by both your shoulders and your feet. Hold the position for as long as you can before dropping your body back down to the floor again.

### Single-leg bridge

This is a variation of the bridge exercise that is slightly more challenging and harder work for your core. Keeping your feet flat on the floor, slowly raise your bottom off the ground so that your weight is supported by your shoulders and feet. Slowly raise and extend one leg while keeping your pelvis raised and level. Try to maintain a straight line from your shoulders to your extended leg and hold for as long as you can. Repeat with the opposite leg.

### Scissor

Lie on your back on an exercise mat with your legs straight. Lift both legs off the ground. Lift your right leg as high as you can, keeping it straight, while stretching your left leg out in front of you, parallel to the floor. Hold this position and then switch legs repeatedly so that both legs are always off the floor.

### Opposite arm and leg raises

This exercise works the abdominals, lower back, gluteal muscles, quadriceps and hamstrings.

On an exercise mat, get down on your hands and knees with your hands directly under your shoulders and your knees directly under your hips. Holding your spine in a straight, neutral position, raise your right arm and left leg simultaneously. Hold for 10 seconds before returning to the starting position, then repeat with the opposite arm and leg.

## Twist

Sit on an exercise mat with your back straight and knees bent. Your torso should be at a 45° angle to the ground. Take a medicine ball and hold the ball with both hands slightly away from your torso. Keeping your feet together, lift both feet off the floor and hold them there. Holding the ball, move it from one side back to the centre and then to the other side, using a twisting motion from the abdomen. This motion should be done continuously or the effect it has on the abdominal muscles will be lost.

## Wide-leg sit-up

Lie down on an exercise mat with your feet more than shoulder width apart. Slowly sit up, lifting your left arm above your head pointing towards the ceiling. Then reach your left arm across your body to touch your right foot. Return to the starting position and repeat with the opposite arm. Continue for as many repetitions as required for your workout.

# PLYOMETRICS

Plyometrics is a type of training that is used by athletes across many different sports. It is designed to produce fast and powerful 'explosive' movements by increasing the speed and force of muscle contractions. Plyometric exercises enable the muscles to reach their maximum force in the shortest amount of time possible. Plyometric exercises are exercises that involve leaping, jumping or hopping movements. They have been used widely since the 1960s to enhance athletes' running speed, jumping ability and general agility to improve overall athleticism.

### How to do plyometric exercises

Plyometric exercises can be done in different forms. They can take the form of: single effort jumps, which are performed once before resetting and repeating; multiple jumps, which are a quick succession of jumps repeated a certain number of times; standing jumps that can be done moving in any direction; and static jumps where you land in the same place you take off from. Plyometric exercises can be combined and made into sequences to train sport-specific movements. For example a 'speed skater' followed by a lateral jump.

### Plyometrics for roller derby

One of the benefits of plyometric training is that it has been found to reduce the incidence of anterior cruciate ligament (ACL) injuries in female athletes, which are common in roller derby. By performing plyometric exercises, you can train your body to perform fast, explosive movements specific to your sport. I will recommend a few exercises here that are specific to training for roller derby.

### Safety for plyometric training

It is often advised that anyone embarking on a plyometric training routine has a good level of fitness and general health. If you do not feel at a high enough level of fitness to start an intense plyometric workout, try building a few off-skates plyometric exercises into your training and slowly build up from there.

### Safety tips

- Plyometric training is a very intense form of training, so in order to do any sort of plyometric training, you must be confident that you are in good health.

- It is not advisable to engage in plyometric exercise if you are in any way injured as they are very intense movments that can put a lot of stress onto joints and ligaments.

- A certain level of fitness, core strength and flexibility is needed to begin plyometric training. If in any doubt that you are able to do so, consult a fitness professional before embarking on any plyometric training programme.

- Build up your training slowly in terms of duration, intensity and frequency – doing too much too soon can result in injury.

- Always warm up, cool down and stretch after training.

- Plyometric exercises must be executed using proper technique at all times, it is better to do fewer repetitions that are well executed than more repetitions with poor form.

- Plyometric training should be supported by adequate nutrition, rest and recovery.

- Plyometric exercises can be performed at a lower volume and intensity by those at a beginner level.

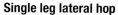

## Plyometric exercises

### Speed skater's exercise

Stand on an exercise mat with your feet hip-width apart. Jump as far as you can to your right, landing on your right leg. Bend your right knee as you land to reduce the impact on your right knee and cross your left leg behind your right, as if you were doing a crossover motion on skates. Then jump as far as you can to your left, landing on your left foot and cross your right leg behind your left. Repeat as many times as required for your workout.

### Single leg lateral hop

This exercise will improve speed, balance and agility, while also strengthening all the muscles that support the knee, hip, ankle, as well as the core. Stand on an exercise mat with your feet hip-width apart. Hop to the side then back to the starting position. Continuously hop for 30 seconds, then repeat on the other leg.

## Squat jumps

The squat jump is the plyometric version of the regular squat. Stand on an exercise mat with your legs hip-width apart and your toes pointing forward. Squat down, bending your knees and reaching your hips back as if to sit down in a chair behind you. Jump straight up as high as you can, landing back in the same place. Bend your knees as you land to protect your joints. Repeat as many times as required for your workout.

## Jumping lunges

The jumping lunge is the plyometric version of a regular lunge. Stand on an exercise mat with your feet hip-width apart. Step forward with your left leg, bending your front knee at a 90° angle. Your right leg should stand directly under your body with your shin parellel to the floor. Jump straight up off the ground and switch your feet in mid air and land in the mirror image of your starting position with your right leg bending forwards and your left leg behind. Bend your knees to absorb the impact when you land. Jump off the ground again and return to the starting position, then repeat as many times as needed for your workout.

## Standing lateral jump

Stand on an exercise mat with your feet hip-width apart. Jump as far as you can to one side and land on both feet with your knees bent to absorb the impact. Return to the starting position and then jump to the other side. Repeat as many times as required for your workout.

## Wide lateral leaps

Stand at the top end of an exercise mat with your feet hip-width apart. Jump as far as you can to your right while travelling forward and land on your right leg bending your right knee as you land to reduce the impact on your knee. Then jump as far as you can to your left whilst travelling forward and land on your left leg. Repeat once more on each leg and then do the exercise in reverse, moving backwards.

# RESISTANCE TRAINING

Research into the benefits of plyometric training has shown that the greatest effectiveness is achieved when plyometric training is done simultaneously with resistance training. The combination of strength training with plyometrics will allow the most explosive power of movement to be achieved. Whether you choose to do this in the same workout or in different workouts is up to you. Everyone is different and you have to decide what is best for you.

### What is resistance training?

The main principle behind resistance training is that you 'overload' the body, forcing it to work harder than it normally would resulting in an improvement in fitness as the body adapts itself to be able to cope with this overloading. The body, in turn, learns to cope with the overload so that it can perform the same task with less effort the next time. This adaptation takes places during the recovery period between workouts. When doing resistance training, you make your muscles work against an opposing force that resists against the muscles you are working. Resistance training is often thought of as weight training, but you can do a complete resistance workout without touching any weights.

### The benefits of resistance training

Resistance training can improve your overall strength and fitness for playing roller derby. It will increase muscle strength and endurance, as well as bone density. It also raises your metabolic rate and is an effective way of building muscle and reducing body fat and cholesterol.

### How to do resistance training

In order to see the benefits of resistance training and see a progression in the positive effects, it is necessary to sustain the effort levels by increasing the duration, frequency and intensity of the exercises and keeping on doing them over a sustained period of time.

You can also do plyometric training with resistance. Do a 'super set' consisting of a heavy resistance exercise with a weighted plyometric exercise: for example squats mixed with weighted squat jumps.

Resistance training will increase muscular strength and endurance – both beneficial for playing roller derby.

In order to experience the benefits of resistance training, it is necessary of increase the duration, frequency and intensity of the exercises over an extended period of time.

## Resistance exercises
### Push-up

Also known as the press-up, this is possibly the most classic of all strength-training exercises. This exercise develops your upper body and core strength, particularly the pectoral muscles, biceps and triceps.

Lie on the floor on your front with your hands directly under your shoulders. Place your toes on top of the exercise ball. Resting your feet on the exercise ball, raise your body off the floor using your arms so that the only contact with the floor is made with your hands. Your body should be in a flat, straight line. Pull in all your core muscles and bend your elbows to lower your shoulders and upper body until your forehead and nose are almost touching the floor, while maintaining a straight back. Straighten your elbows to raise yourself and repeat as many times as required for your workout. This exercise can also be done with the feet resting on the floor.

### Barbell squat

This exercise is best performed inside a squat rack for safety purposes. Put the bar on a rack to just below shoulder level and load the bar with a weight you feel confident you are able to lift safely. Step under the bar and position yourself with the back of your shoulders across it and the bar slightly below your neck.

Hold the bar using both arms at each side and push with your legs and at the same time straighten your torso to lift the bar off the rack. Step away from the rack and position your feet hip width apart. Slowly lower the bar by bending your knees, keeping your back straight and your head up. Continue to squat down until the angle between your thighs and calves is at slightly less than 90°. Raise the bar by pushing the floor with the heel of your foot as you straighten the legs and return to the starting position. Repeat as many times as required for your workout.

## Barbell deadlift

Stand with your feet hip-width apart in front of a loaded barbell. Bend your knees and bend forward, keeping your back as straight as possible. Hold onto the bar with both hands shoulder-width apart using an overhand grip. This will be the starting position of the exercise. Lift the bar by pushing with your legs while simultaneously lifting your torso to the upright position, keeping your back straight at all times. In the upright position, stick your chest out and contract the back by bringing the shoulder blades back. Bend your knees while simultaneously leaning the torso forward at the waist to return to the starting position, keeping the back straight at all times. Place the bar back onto the floor and repeat as many times as required for your workout.

## Dumb-bell lunges

Holding a dumb-bell in each hand with your arms resting by your sides, step forward with your left leg and squat down through your hips, bending your front knee at a 90° angle. Your right leg should stand directly under your body with your shin parallel to the floor. Push up using the heel of your foot and go back to the starting position. Repeat as many times as required for your workout and then perform with the other leg.

# SKATER PROFILE *TRIPLE SHOT MISTO, ROCKY MOUNTAIN ROLLERGIRLS, COLORADO, USA*

**How long have you been playing roller derby?**
Two years.

**Did you skate before you started playing roller derby?**
Yes, since I could walk.

**Did you play any other sports before you started playing roller derby?**
Skiing and snowboarding since the age of five; swimming, gymnastics and dance as a child; running – for more than 15 years; triathlons (three years); adventure racing (four years).

**How has roller derby affected your overall health and fitness?**
Roller derby has greatly improved my overall stability, balance, agility, cardio endurance, as well as my sprinting, muscle strength and athletic confidence.

**How often do you practise on skates?**
Three times a week for three hours.

**What other off-skates training do you do and how often?**
I exercise every day. This usually includes an hour of cardio and then an hour of yoga, Pilates, and/or strength training.

**Which other sports support roller derby?**
Skiing uses the same leg muscles; roller and ice hockey are very aggressive and fast-paced sports; running utilises sprinting and interval spurts; American football is a full-contact sport with blockers and plays reminiscent of derby; biking uses a lot of the same muscles and incorporates constant intervals.

**What type of training has helped you to improve most as a skater?**
Interval sprinting and cardio training in addition to yoga for increased balance and agility.

**What advice would you give new skaters about training for roller derby?**
Work on your endurance. It is key to improving in every other aspect of the game!

**What would you recommend doing to prevent injuries?**
Cross train your ass off! Focus especially on strengthening the knees and ankles!

**How has playing roller derby affected your lifestyle?**
I give up a lot of time with my family: I have three kids and derby has taken away countless 'school-night' quality hours with them. But, it's all worth it! I love the sport, I love the other athletic women I have met playing this game, I love pushing myself, I love having something that I'm doing solely for me! Derby has made me more confident, more accepting and more competitive! It's also taught me to appreciate life and where I dedicate my time. It's taught me to respect my body and be confident in who I am. I also think it's been great for my kids to see their mom work hard for something and see the importance of sports and health throughout one's life.

# SKATER PROFILE *RAT-A-TAT KAT,*
## *GOTHAM GIRLS ROLLER DERBY, NEW YORK*

### Did you skate before you started playing roller derby?

I skated with a little club here in Brooklyn called Sweet Action Skate Club. We'd skate parks and the (now defunct) Empire Rink in Crown Heights.

### Did you play any other sports before playing roller derby?

I played a bunch of sports growing up. I grew up on horses, competing from the age of seven through college doing hunter/jumper. I played soccer for most of my youth and did field hockey and lacrosse through high school. My field hockey team won the State Championships my sophomore year.

### How has playing roller derby affected your overall health and fitness?

I honestly think that roller derby has put me in the best shape that I've ever been in. I used to run a lot, which gave me a lot of conditioning, but we do so much cross-training in derby that I feel like overall, my body is the best shape it's ever been in. Not bad, seeing that I'm in my 30s! I feel strong and resilient, and look pretty good walking down the street, if I do say so myself!

### How often do you practise on skates?

Three to four times a week. We have league practice twice a week, Bronx practice once a week, while Traitors (our B-team) practise once a week.

### What additional off-skates training do you do and how often?

I do pilates once a week, and go for bike rides several times a week. Pilates has improved my balance and alignment, which can get really wacky from going one way around the track.

### Which other sports do you think support playing roller derby?

I'm really impressed with the diversity of athletic backgrounds that our skaters bring to the table. I think that almost any sport can help with derby. They build discipline, and instil an understanding and appreciation of fitness, even if it's just basic. We have former figure skaters and ice hockey players, but also soccer champions, fitness instructors, and tae kwon do black belts! They each provide value in their own ways, and we try to harvest these individuals' strengths as a league.

For example, you might find it hard to see the connection between derby and my horse riding background, but there is one. You need confidence and dedication to be out there jumping fences on a 1500 pound animal, and require a willingness to adjust to new challenges as they come. You and your horse need to rely on each other just as much as you need to rely on your 13 other teammates in roller derby. And nothing – absolutely nothing – prepares you better for the bumps and full-on smackdowns of roller derby than being thrown into a few fences!

### What type of training has helped you to improve most as a skater?

As I mentioned before, I really think that my Pilates training has helped me with my core strength and balance. Oh, and endurance training. I *hate* a lot of the endurance stuff that we do, like sprints, etc. But I know that they are good for me, so I suck it up.

# CROSS-TRAINING

Using other sports is another great way of training for roller derby. Any other sport you do will be in some way beneficial to your overall fitness but there are some sports that are more relevant to developing certain aspects of fitness specifically for roller derby.

### Benefits of cross-training

There are all sorts of reasons that cross-training using different sports can be beneficial to roller derby and these vary from one sport to another. Cross-training using other sports will not only provide some variation in your roller derby training but it will also balance the amount of strain you are putting on the muscles and joints over-represented playing roller derby by training your body in a different way.

### Yoga

Yoga improves balance, coordination and flexibility, while increasing strength and stretching out all the muscles. It also improves your strength of mind. These are all integral physical attributes to playing roller derby.

## Cycling

A lot of rollergirls swear by cycling. It works all the muscles in the legs, especially the quadriceps, hamstrings, hip flexors and all of the core muscles without putting too much impact on the joints. It is also a form of interval training by default as you are always stopping and starting, going faster and slower and varying incline depending on terrain. For those who aren't able to cycle on a regular basis, spinning classes provide many of the same benefits.

## Pilates

Pilates is great training for roller derby because it really focuses on developing your core strength. It also provides some stretching for flexibility but the core workout gained from Pilates is very beneficial to playing roller derby because having a strong core is essential for to achieving good balance and stability when on skates.

### Boxing and kickboxing

This is great for working on core strength, footwork, contact, agility, speed and explosive power because the biomechanics of boxing are similar to the biomechanics of the contact aspect of roller derby.

### Running

Running is great for endurance and cardiovascular fitness and can also be used as an effective form of interval training.

### Swimming

Swimming is great for building strength, endurance and cardiovascular fitness. It also provides a full-body workout without putting pressure on the joints. Athletes often use swimming as a method of rehabilitation after injury.

### Skiing and snowboarding

Skiing and snowboarding are great for balance, endurance and explosive strength in all the right muscle groups for playing roller derby. The optimum position in skiing or snowboarding is very similar to derby position.

### Ice skating or in-line skating

Any other type of skating will provide great cross-training for roller derby. Although different types of skating use balance a little differently depending on the skates used, all types of skating provide great training for balance, coordination, agility and proprioception.

### Ice hockey

Ice hockey is another high-speed contact sport played on skates. It involves all of the same skills as roller derby and includes the same element of contact where players 'body check' each other while they are skating.

### Speed skating

Regularly practising speed skating will train endurance, cardiovascular fitness and, of course, speed. It is a great way to develop correct form and technique while skating, to achieve as much speed as possible with your stride.

# Looking after
# your body

# INJURIES

Roller derby is an uncompromising contact sport so injuries can, and do, happen. Bumps, bruises and scrapes are all commonplace, but sometimes more serious injuries occur, even to the very best of skaters. It is very important for every skater to look after their body as best they can in order to prevent injuries from happening.

## Causes of injuries

The most common cause of injury is, of course, falling. Falling in roller derby is inevitable, even for the most stable of skaters, because playing roller derby involves full contact at high speed. Protective gear such as helmets, knee and elbow pads and wrist guards can only protect the skaters up to a point, and sometimes players endure sprains, strains, torn ligaments and even broken bones.

Because roller derby is a very physically demanding sport where skaters are doing a lot of training, overworked and fatigued muscles are also common, which is why it is always important to supplement training with proper diet and adequate amounts of rest and recovery.

The most common injuries occur to the joints and muscles that are worked the most. Strained quadriceps and hamstrings are common, as well as sprained ankles and torn ligaments in the knees. Injuries to the upper body are less common but also occur, as the wrists and shoulders are also vulnerable when falling.

## Common causes of injuries

- Poor alignment
- Discrepancy in leg length
- Muscle weakness or imbalance
- Decreased flexibility
- Joint hyperlaxity
- Age, poor general health, obesity
- Training errors, too much, too-fast progression, fatigue, poor technique
- Bad conditions
- Poor safety equipment

Roller derby is a frenetic contact sport and the skaters are at risk of injury. Knees and ankles are particularly vulnerable.

# SKATER PROFILE: *ISABELLE RINGER, SAN DIEGO DERBY DOLLS, CALIFORNIA, USA*

**How long have you been playing roller derby?**
I joined the San Diego Derby Dolls in February of 2006.

**Did you skate before you started roller derby?**
I would occasionally go to the roller rink with friends in my adolescent years, but I was never any good. I spent the first several years of my roller derby career learning to skate well enough to actually start working on learning the technique and strategy of the game.

**Did you play any other sports before you started roller derby?**
When I was a kid, I swam year-round from ages eight to18. Unfortunately I peaked somewhere around 11 or 12 years old so I never pursued the sport any further after high school. I also dabbled in many other sports in my early childhood though thinned it down to swimming, soccer and some track and field in high school.

**How has roller derby affected your overall health and fitness?**
I started roller derby because I needed to get a little more fitness in my life. I was in my mid-twenties, hated going to the gym and really needed a physical outlet. When a co-worker of my husband's mentioned she was playing I figured I'd go out and give it a try. Little did I know that, years later, I would be going back to the gym to get better at the sport. Now I am really into health and fitness because I want to be a better roller derby player. It seems a bit ironic.

**How often do you practise on skates?**
Generally when we are in-season, which is virtually all year, I attend various practices three to four days per week. I generally put in around eight to ten hours in an average week on skates.

**What additional off-skates training do you do and how often?**
This really depends on where I'm at in the season. For example, from January 1 of this year I did a serious 90-day training regime to get fit for the new season. Ideally I'd love to be getting in a 45-minute off-skates workout three days a week. It's so easy to make excuses about why you're too busy for it. That's why a set regime really helped me.

**What type of training has helped you to improve the most as a skater?**
For me, off-skates core work made a huge difference in my game. As soon as I got stronger, I was able to clean up my game quite a bit and start learning some more advanced stuff. I did an intense training programme called P90X. I got amazing results and 90 days is a short time to see a noticeable difference. The programme works different muscle groups every day so you're always changing up your workout. It was hard, but it was manageable. I actually spent a few less hours at roller derby practice and a few more hours each week doing my off-skates training over those 90 days.

**What advice would you give to new skaters about training for roller derby?**
Many skaters come into derby on a recreational level and then get bitten by the bug and want to be great at the sport, which is so rad! However, it takes a certain level of fitness to be able to give a hit and skate away and to be able to sit down into your stride and really push and pull with power strokes. You will eventually get

there if you really want it, even if you don't do off-skates training. It just helps expedite the process. Everyone wants to get better faster, that's one way you can.

### Have you sustained any injuries playing roller derby?

Yes. I tore my ACL (anterior cruciate ligament) in September 2009 and had to have full reconstructive surgery in December. It's really what inspired me to start paying more attention to my workout and diet and get fit so hopefully I won't find myself in that situation again. When I came back from that injury, I was a much better skater. So though it was pretty miserable at the time, I was able to get something really positive out of it in the long run.

### What did you do to aid your recovery and get back to training?

My orthopedic surgeon got me into physical therapy right away after surgery. I was an excellent patient. I did everything my doctor asked, every exercise my therapist recommended, and then when I came back to practice, I'd have everyone do all my physical therapy exercises too so that they'd get stronger with me.

### What would you recommend doing as a skater to prevent injuries?

Knees are made up of a lot of ligaments that are like elastic bands. You really don't want to have that elastic get too stretched out or twisted up. So the more work your muscles can do, the less work all those little fragile parts have to. Roller derby players overall could use more hamstring workouts. We have really developed quads but our hamstrings are not balanced out at all for the vast majority of us. Your hamstrings do a very similar job as your ACL so if your hamstring is really strong, your ACL doesn't have to do so much work.

Secondly, get good kneepads from the get-go and wear them every time you skate. We fall so much in this sport and you only get one body to work with. Once you trash it, you can't trade it in for a new one.

# PREVENTING INJURIES

As with any sport, it is impossible to prepare for or prevent every possible injury. However, there are a few things you can do to keep yourself safer and reduce the risk of getting hurt. Prevention is always better than cure, and there are several simple things you can do to help prevent injuries from happening on the track.

- Always wear suitable clothing and protective gear. Make sure your pads, helmet and mouth guard fit correctly and buy the highest quality you can afford so that you know your body is well protected.
- Make sure you are hydrated enough to play and always have enough water with you to ensure you don't get dehydrated.
- Always warm up and cool down properly before and after any exercise.
- Make sure you get enough rest and recovery time between training. Muscles that are tense and fatigued are much more prone to pulls and tears.
- Stretch well after every training session.
- Work on your technique. Good technique in every type of training is key to injury prevention. Whether it is your skating or blocking technique, your form in plyometric or resistance training, sloppy technique, poor form or carelessness can lead to injuries.
- Push yourself within reason but always train at a level that is safe for you.
- If you experience any undue pain beyond a little muscle stiffness or soreness while training it is best to stop and seek medical advice before continuing.
- Proper nutrition and diet will mean that your body has enough fuel for exercise and is able to recover properly from any training you are doing.
- Muscle conditioning, flexibility and proprioceptive training will all help to better prepare your body to prevent injuries.

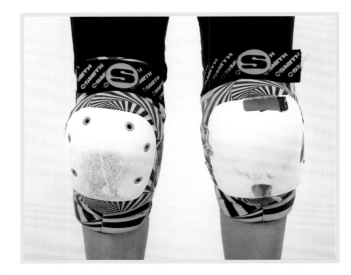

High-quality protective gear including knee and elbow pads, wrist guards, helmet and mouth guard are essential for preventing injuries. Remember to replace your pads regularly to ensure that you are protected properly.

## Warming up

Warming up before you begin is essential for doing any exercise safely. It raises the body temperature and lubricates the joints, stimulates the blood flow to the muscles and makes them easier to stretch. It is better to warm up before stretching or doing exercise because stretching cold muscles can do more harm than good. The body performs more efficiently when warm so an athlete's performance will actually improve after a good warm-up. A good warm-up will also prepare you psychologically to perform well in a game or even in a training session. Warm up before training by skating or jogging gently for at least 5–10 minutes before stretching or beginning to exercise, the amount of time and intensity of the warm up needed will vary from person to person depending on individual level of fitness.

## Cooling down

The cool down after exercise is just as important as the warm-up before, some would say even more so.

The muscles are much more likely to become stiff if hard exercise is suddenly stopped with no period of cooling down. The cool-down can also reduce the muscle ache that many athletes experience after vigorous training.

Hard training can cause local swelling within a muscle, which causes delayed-onset muscle soreness, also known as DOMS. This is where you feel fine the day after training but very sore or stiff the following day. To reduce the effects of DOMS, you should perform a warm down using similar exercises to your warm up then gradually lowering the intensity until you reach a resting position.

## Joint care

Roller derby is very tough on the joints, particularly the knees. Falling on your knees can take its toll so you may wish to take some supplements to aid recovery and healthy functioning of the joints. Glucosamine and condroitin has been found to be very helpful in helping with joint recovery and protection. However, glucosamine is derived from shellfish, so if you are a vegetarian, hyaluronic acid can be takens, which does not contain animal products.

## Overtraining

Many athletes experience fatigue and this often results in a failure to recover from the stresses placed on the body during training. This is known as overtraining and, in severe cases, can lead to a state of prolonged fatigue and underperformance. It is caused by training too hard without enough rest. To prevent this from happening, always make sure you have adequate rest and recovery time between training, good diet and enough sleep.

Make sure your pads, helmet and mouth guard all fit correctly. Ill-fitting protective gear can leave you vulnerable to injuries.

# SKATER PROFILE *EM DASH, GOTHAM GIRLS ROLLER DERBY, NEW YORK, USA*

**How long have you been playing roller derby?**
Since July 2007

**Did you skate before you started roller derby?**
I played ice hockey and roller bladed, but I never skated on quads before I became interested in roller derby.

**Did you play any other sports before you started roller derby?**
I played many sports before roller derby, but the most important were: ice hockey, six years; softball, more than eight years; skiing, since I was three or four; volleyball, three years.

**How has roller derby affected your overall health and fitness?**
I'm definitely in much better shape than I was before derby. That said, I tend to be injured and in pain a lot more than I was before I started playing derby. I guess it comes with the territory of being a serious athlete.

**How often do you practise on skates?**
Three to four times a week.

**What additional off-skates training do you do and how often?**
I jog and bike, depending on the season, but not on a set schedule. I also try to do off-skates strengthening like push-ups, crunches and squats every day I don't have practice.

**What advice would you give to new skaters about training for roller derby?**
Everything you do to get more fit (without burning yourself out) will help with derby, but you don't have to start out jumping up stairs for an hour. It's OK to start slow. If you can't do 10 good pushups, do one. Then do two the next day. Every day, push yourself a little farther.

**Have you sustained any injuries playing roller derby?**
Lots. I separated my AC (acromioclavicular) joint in my shoulder and partially tore my labrum, I had a bone bruise on one hip, I've got bursitis and tendonitis from bad falls on both my knees, I had sesamoiditis (an aggravated bone/tendon in my foot) this past year that forced me to wear a walking cast for five weeks. Plus tons of smaller bumps and bruises.

**What did you do to aid your recovery and get back to training?**
I always try to do all the exercises my physical therapist recommends, but I also try to take the time I need to really heal. The last thing I want is to sit out a second time because I've rushed back to skating before I was ready. I'm only 28, and I want to have these knees, shoulders, feet, etc. for a long, long time.

**What would you recommend doing to prevent injuries?**
Off-skates strengthening and cross-training can help prevent injuries from happening, and make it easier to recover once they do. And invest in good pads! Good safety gear is expensive, but not nearly as expensive as all the doctors' visits and physical therapy that goes with any injury.

# SKATER PROFILE *PIPPI STRONGSOCKING, GOTHAM GIRLS ROLLER DERBY, NEW YORK, USA*

***How long have you been playing roller derby?***
Two years

***Did you skate before playing roller derby?***
I started skating in June 2009 before try-outs in December 2009. Before and after work in the dinner parking lot by my house and on the weekends at every skate rink in the tri-state area.

***Did you play any other sports before you started playing roller derby?***
Not really ... I had metal clip-on skates when I was a kid and some gym-shoe skates in the late 1970s that I loved to skate around in. I played some organised sports like softball and soccer but I sucked and I didn't fit in with the jock girls. I'm super competitive so I would play everyone in my neighbourhood to the death at tether ball or kick the can ... finally I had to start to play with the high school kids when I was eight because kids my age couldn't take my mean streak.

***How has playing roller derby affected your overall health and fitness?***
I have a herniated disc in my lower back that was crippling before derby. Believe me when I say derby cured me! It's all core work and now I'm strong and stable!

***How often do you practise on skates?***
I go to the two league practices offered, my home team practice, Men's team practice, speed skating and then I skate to the grocery store and I wear skates when I rake the leaves in my backyard to practice my agility. I'm a bit obsessed.

***Which other sports support roller derby?***
Speed-skating and hockey. Though roller derby is really getting girls interested in sports. It's unlike any other sport. You can look cool and be tough as nails without compromising your femininity.

***What type of training has helped you to improve most as a skater?***
Time on my skates helps me. Speed skating helps tremendously. It's lots of endurance and tiny skills that improve your form and make you skate more efficiently.

***What advice would you give to new skaters about fitness/training for roller derby?***
One thing you can control is your fitness level. If you smoke ... quit! If you eat junk food ... stop! Derby is becoming seriously competitive. Nobody likes to lose. If you have done all you can to live and train as an athlete then you can be proud of what happens on the track. You're only doing your team a disservice if you slack.

# STRETCHING

Stretching before and after exercise is vital to any athlete's training programme. It improves the overall flexibility and suppleness of the muscles, as well as preparing them for physical exertion and promoting recovery, generally lessening your chances of unnecessary injury.

### Why stretching is important

Roller derby has the reputation of being a very dangerous sport where a lot of injuries happen, and there are definitely risks involved. In playing roller derby our lower limbs have to tolerate a lot of stress with every stride, so being strong and supple is essential for dealing with the strain that roller derby puts on your muscles.

### Reducing muscle tightness

It is very important to stretch the whole body with particular emphasis on the leg muscles so that they don't become excessively tight. If the leg muscles are tight, there is more risk of pulling the soft tissue areas around the knees and ankles. It is also important to keep the surrounding muscles strong so that the pelvis, knees and ankles are well supported.

### Should you stretch before or after exercise?

Experts in sports science endlessly debate the need to stretch before and after exercise and whether it is beneficial or not. This information can be very confusing. However, recent research has shown that dynamic stretching is most beneficial before training as it will better prepare your body for exercise, and static stretching is better after training in order to aid recovery. Static stretching between training sessions, or practising yoga regularly, will also help to promote overall flexibility.

### Muscles to stretch for roller derby

It's worth doing a full-body stretch with particular emphasis on the following muscles:
• Quadriceps
• Hamstrings
• Calves
• Hip adductors
• Hip abductors
• Hip flexors
• Gluteal muscles
• Lower back

There are many different types of stretches you can do on these muscles and this book will only recommend a few. It really comes down to personal preference, so you should choose your own routine for stretching and find out what works best for you.

### Dynamic stretching

Recent research has shown that dynamic stretching before exercise is more effective in preparing the body for exercise and preventing injury, reducing soreness of the muscles and improving flexibility and athletic performance. Dynamic stretching should use sport-specific movements to prepare your body from the particular type of activity to follow the stretching.

### Stretching before the game

In roller derby, the best way to stretch dynamically before a game is to perform a series of dynamic stretches on skates, which take the body through some of the movements used during the game to prepare the body for the motions it will need to endure. Movements such as squatting down and standing up again, lifting the knees, swinging the legs outward in front, behind and to each side are examples of many different motions you can do.

# DYNAMIC STRETCHES WITH KAMIKAZE KITTEN

These are basic dynamic stretches we used to warm up for roller derby. Many of these were taught to me by the lovely skaters at Auckland Roller Derby – so thanks a lot ARDL!

The key when executing these movements is keeping control and gradually increasing the range of motion in the limbs and joints. I usually perform them skating around the track, either forwards or backwards, and insert a lap of low squat stance between each set.

A set is performing the full movement 10 times. The motion should be fluid and constant rather than held in a static pose.

### Knee raises

Start to wake up your hip flexors by raising your knee up as you skate. Do this 10 times for each leg. With the first few you won't get your knee to hip level, but your knee should get higher each time.

**Primary muscles activated:** hip flexors, quadriceps, hamstrings.

### Butt kicks

Next warm up the hamstrings and stretch out the quads with some butt kicks. Raise your heel up behind you 10 times for each foot. Try to keep your knee pointing at the floor rather than pointing backwards.

**Primary muscles activated:** gluteus maximus, quadriceps, hamstrings.

### Leg swings

This is a similar motion to the previous stretches but is more intense because of the straight leg. Swing your leg forwards and backwards, getting as much motion in the hips as you comfortably can.

**Primary muscles activated:** gluteus maximus, hip flexors, quadriceps, hamstrings.

## Hip openers and hip closers

It's really important to get your hips warmed up before skating, especially if you use the side-surfing position to execute hits or move around the track. Our bodies are so used to the front-to-back motion of our legs that the muscles used to turn the knees to the side are often underused and shortened.

Raise your knee up, open it outwards, drop it down with the foot pointing out to the side and then raise it back up again in a circular motion. Repeat 10 times on each leg. Follow with hip closers, which use the same motion but in the opposite direction.
**Primary muscles activated:** all muscles of the hips.

## Thumbs up

In order to get some more heat into the shoulders, rotator cuff, deltoids and trapezius, hold your arms out straight to the sides level with your shoulders. Have one thumb pointing upwards, and the other thumb pointing downwards. Twist your thumbs up and down whilst maintaining the tension and control through your arms.
**Primary muscles activated:** rotator cuff, deltoids, trapezius.

## Ankle rotation

With a straight leg raised off the ground, point your toe and rotate your ankle in clockwise circles. Aim to keep the motion smooth and controlled. These probably won't be the perfect circles you imagine when you first start doing them until you have built up the flexibility and strength in your ankle. Do 10 circles on each foot and then repeat, rotating in the opposite direction.

**Primary muscles activated:** complex muscles of the ankle, peroneus longus, peroneus brevis, gastrocnemius, soleus.

## Arm raises

Arm raises aren't for warming up the arms. They are for warming up the shoulders, back and core muscles.

Bring your straight arms behind you as far as you can reach: the more you stretch backwards, the more muscles you'll activate around the scapula. Swing them forwards and up as far over your head as you can reach. The reach at the top should activate the deltoids and the triceps.

**Primary muscles activated:** supraspinatus, deltoid, serratus anterior, latissimus dorsi.

## Arm crosses

Stretch and activate the pectoral muscles and the teres muscles by opening your arms and then crossing them in front of you. It's really important that you don't use the weight of your arms to throw them across your body and that it remains a controlled movement. Repeat 10 times.

**Primary muscles activated:** pectorals, deltoids and teres muscles.

## Full extension

Finish off the stretching with a full movement from compression to extension. Squat down and touch your toe stops then raise upwards until you are reaching as high as possible, before lowering down into a squat again.

**Primary muscles activated:** most of them!

# STATIC STRETCHING

Static stretching is best done after exercise. It involves taking a limb to the point at which tightness is felt and then holding this position. While holding the position, the muscles elongate as muscle reflexes detect tension in the muscle tendon and gradually allow the muscle to relax. To increase the body's flexibility and range of motion, each static stretch can be done with four to five repetitions, with a rest of 10–20 seconds between reps.

Remember to execute each stretch with correct form and only push your body so that the muscles are stretched and not strained.

### Kneeling hamstring stretch
Kneel down on your right knee and extend your left leg in front of you. Keep your back straight as you hold the stretch. Repeat with the opposite leg.

### Calf lunge stretch
Stand on a flat surface with your feet hip-width apart and your toes pointing forward. Extend one leg forward and bend your front knee while keeping both heels on the floor. Shift your weight forward over your front knee to deepen the stretch and hold for up to 30 seconds, keeping your back leg straight. Make sure the body is aligned and the spine straight while executing this stretch. Repeat with the opposite leg.

## Standing quad stretch

Stand with you feet hip-width apart and hold onto a chair to help you balance. Grab your left foot with your left hand. Keep your thighs lined up next to each other with the left leg in line with the hip. Hold the stretch for up to 30 seconds, then repeat with the opposite leg.

## Hip flexor stretch

Kneel down on an exercise mat. Step forward with your right foot, keeping your left knee on the floor. Tighten your abdominal muscles and keep your back straight. Press forward and push your hip into extension. Hold for 30 seconds and then repeat with the opposite leg in front.

## Lying gluteal stretch

Lie down on your back on an exercise mat. Bend one leg with your foot resting on the floor. Straighten your other leg and raise it towards the ceiling. Cross your bent leg over your straight leg and rest the foot of the bent leg on the thigh of the straight leg. Pull your straight leg towards your chest and hold for up to 30 seconds, then repeat with the opposite leg.

## Hip flexors and extensors and gluteal muscles

Start standing on an exercise mat with your feet hip width apart. Step forwards with your left leg and lower yourself to the ground, supporting your bodyweight with your hands. Turn your left knee outwards and your left foot inwards to bring the left thigh down to the ground. At the same time, slide your right leg backwards to bring it down onto the mat. Lean forward to increase the stretch and hold for up to 30 seconds, then repeat with the opposite leg.

## Back flexion stretch

On an exercise mat, get down on your hands and knees with your hands directly under your shoulders and your knees directly under your hips. Round your spine by pushing your back up towards the ceiling and tucking your tailbone under until you feel a stretch. Hold for up to 30 seconds and return to the starting position.

## Back extension stretch

This stretch can be directly linked to the back flexion stretch. After returning to the starting position, arch your back and extend your spine, pointing your tailbone towards the ceiling. Hold for up to 30 seconds and return to the starting position.

## Spinal rotation stretch

Lie down on your back on an exercise mat. Flex your left knee and cross it over your right leg, bringing your left knee down towards the floor. Rotate your torso towards your right leg and hold the stretch for up to 30 seconds. Repeat on the other side.

# SKATER PROFILE *FRAK ATTACK, ROCKY MOUNTAIN ROLLERGIRLS, COLORADO, USA*

**How long have you been playing roller derby?**
Two years and some change.

**Did you skate before you started roller derby?**
I was briefly a rink rat when I was a kid and played roller hockey well into middle school.

**Did you play any other sports before you started roller derby?**
I did a lot of track when younger, hitting in late middle school and all through high school and at college I played competitive volleyball.

**How has roller derby affected your overall health and fitness?**
It's made me more conscious of my health and fitness, where I need to drive it to and what I need to do to maintain it. I've been more willing to put effort into it instead of just doing it for the cosmetic benefits.

**How often do you practise on skates?**
Two to three times a week on average.

**What other off-skates training do you do and how often?**
As much as I can fit into my schedule! Weight training, plyometrics, endurance, boxing, cardio and yoga. Anything that I feel will help me with my fitness. It's anywhere between three to five days a week for about an hour.

**Which other sports support roller derby?**
Hockey and speed skating seem to be the most obvious, but I've seen so many gals with different sport backgrounds: from boxing to rugby to martial arts.

**What type of training has helped you to improve most as a skater?**
Boxing was doing a great job with my ability to take hits and give hits. Though basic physical therapy, including strengthening and stability exercises have done wonders.

**Have you sustained any injuries playing roller derby?**
The most serious to date is a type 2 PCL tear (posterior cruciate ligament) and meniscus tear.

**What did you do to aid your recovery and get back to training?**
I followed my doctor, chiropractor and physical therapist's orders to a tee. I did not give way to my want to skate despite how frustrating it was. I followed every exercise, pushed as hard as I could so long as there was no pain. But I was also very persistent in talking to them about when I could start to do certain things. When I was allowed to start biking and using the elliptical trainer, I was on them every day. When I could start doing yoga, I was there every week. I also stopped drinking to help focus on my health and injury: it's possible it did very little, but it did make me feel great! There is also a point where you have to find the balance between pushing it and stopping. The best advice I ever got was, sharp pain or growing pain, you're done.

### What would you recommend doing to prevent injuries?

Strengthening exercises! They were a life-saver in my recovery and I wish I had focused on them before it happened. But also, listening to your body. I didn't the first time around, and when I went back after two weeks of initial injury, I hurt it more and was out for six months. Listen to what your body has to say and if you have access to chiropractors, orthopaedics and any medical staff, use them! They are the best support system a skater can have.

# COMMON INJURIES IN ROLLER DERBY

The following section looks at the most usual injuries likely to be encountered in roller derby and how to prevent and treat them, including soft tissue damage and tears, sprains and other problems with tendons and ligaments.

## Soft tissue injuries

Soft tissue injuries and inflammation affect the muscles, tendons and fascia (connective tissue). If you experience sore muscles or inflammation these can be treated by resting and applying ice to the affected area to reduce inflammation. Inflamed joints or limbs can be supported with an elastic bandage to add compression to reduce the swelling.

## Knee injuries

Knee injuries can generally be divided into acute knee injuries and overuse knee injuries.

Acute knee injuries include knee sprain (including

torn or ruptured knee ligaments such as the ACL), torn meniscus, or knee cartilage, ruptured knee tendon and knee fracture in very sever cases. Knee overuse injuries include knee tendonitis, knee bursitis, iliotibial band syndrome and muscle strains.

The two main muscle groups that control knee movement and stability are the quadriceps and the hamstrings. The quadriceps run along the front of the thigh and attach to the front of the shinbone, just below the knee. These muscles control the straightening of the knees and the movement of the kneecap. They are used to extend the leg and is one of the main muscle groups used in roller skating.

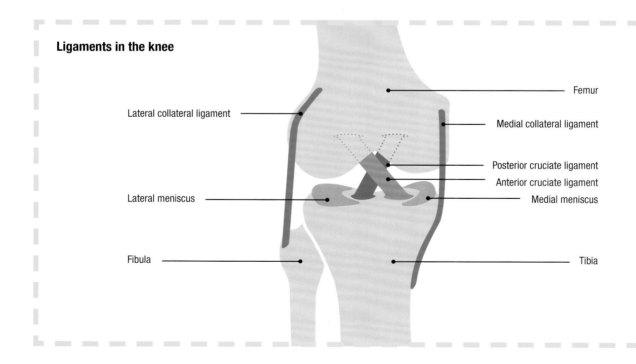

**Ligaments in the knee**

Femur

Lateral collateral ligament

Medial collateral ligament

Posterior cruciate ligament

Anterior cruciate ligament

Lateral meniscus

Medial meniscus

Fibula

Tibia

The hamstrings are the muscles at the back of the thigh that attach the pelvis at the top and the back of the shinbone just below the knee. They are used to bend the knee and are also one of the main muscle groups used in roller skating.

Other muscles that affect the stability of the knee are the calf muscles, hip abductors on the outer thigh and hip adductors on the inner thigh, the iliotibial band, which is the fibrous tissue on the outer thigh from the hip to below the knee, and also the gluteal muscles.

Many knee injuries are the result of a lack of stability in the knee due to an imbalance in the muscles supporting the knee. In some cases, the quadriceps are significantly stronger than the hamstrings which can cause weakness in the knees. In these cases, concentrating on stretching the quadriceps and strengthening the hamstrings can balance out the problem. It is important to strengthen all the muscles that support the knee so as not to create an imbalance.

## ACL injuries

The ACL is the anterior cruciate ligament in the knee. It is located within the capsule of the knee and connects the femur and tibia. The ACL is responsible for limiting rotational movement in the knee joint, as well as restraining excessive forward movement of the tibia.

ACL injuries are the most common injury affecting the knee joint and are one of the most common injuries in roller derby. An ACL injury is the result of excessive stretching or tearing of the ligament. The severity of injury can range from a slight stretching to a complete rupture.

### Causes of ACL injuries in roller derby
- A twisting motion at the knee joint
- A sudden impact to the front of the knee
- A sudden stop or change of direction or speed

### Treatment
As with any injury, the treatment depends on the severity of the injury sustained. Rest, Ice, Compression and Elevation are recommended as immediate treatment, but always see a doctor to seek proper medical treatment. Very severe ACL injuries such as a complete tear of the ligament are likely to require surgery.

### Preventing ACL injuries
There are several things you can do to help prevent ACL injuries from occurring:

- **Warm up and down** A good warm up is essential to prepare the body for any form of exercise and will prepare the joints, muscles and ligaments for strenuous activity.
- **Stretch** Thoroughly stretching all the muscle groups in the leg to attain maximum flexibility will make it easier for the joints/muscles/ligaments to cope with the strain of exercise.
- **Strengthen** Work on the strength of all the muscles around the knee to ensure they are able to support the joints in the best way possible.
- **Balancing exercises** Balancing exercises can be used to improve proprioception as well as your body's ability to balance. Any exercise that challenges the body's ability to balance will help with this. Training on a balance board can be used for this specific purpose.
- **Stop** If any activities cause you pain or discomfort then stop training or modify the activity and seek medical advice
- **Rest** Rest and recovery are essential for the body's soft tissues to recover from strenuous exercise. Ensure that you allow enough time for your body to recover between training sessions.

## Hamstring injuries

The hamstring is the group of muscles located at the back of the thigh. These muscles are the semimembranosus, semitendinosus and biceps femoris. The tops of these muscles are attached to the lower pelvis and the bottoms of these muscles are attached to the tibia and fibula just below the knee. They are very susceptible to tears and strains, and athletes playing roller derby can often experience these injuries as they are most common in sports that require high speed, power and agility.

### How does a hamstring injury occur?

A hamstring injury is the result of a pulling action that tears or stretches the hamstring muscles or the tendons that attach the muscles to the bones at either end. There are different degrees of severity of hamstring injuries. The first involves a minor stretching of the muscles and tendons and incurs mild pain, swelling and stiffness. The second degree involves both stretching and minor tearing of the muscles and tendons and this results in increased pain, swelling and stiffness. A third-degree strain is the result of a complete tear or rupture of one or more of the tendons or muscles. The result of this is a lot of pain and swelling and instability.

### Causes of hamstring injury in roller derby

- Fatigue – tired hamstring muscles are very susceptible to injury.
- Imbalance in strength between the quadriceps and hamstring muscles: very strong quadriceps and weak hamstrings results in a great amount of pressure being placed on the hamstrings.
- General lack of strength and flexibility in the hamstring muscles.
- Sudden movements that put too much pressure on the hamstrings.

### Preventing hamstring injuries

The best way to prevent hamstring injuries is to stretch and strengthen the hamstring muscles and tendons as much as possible. Increasing the strength and flexibility of the hamstring muscles will enable the muscles and tendons to better resist strains and injuries. Combining regular stretching with cross-training such as cycling, resistance training and plyometrics is the best way to prepare the hamstrings for playing roller derby.

**The main muscles in the legs used in playing roller derby**

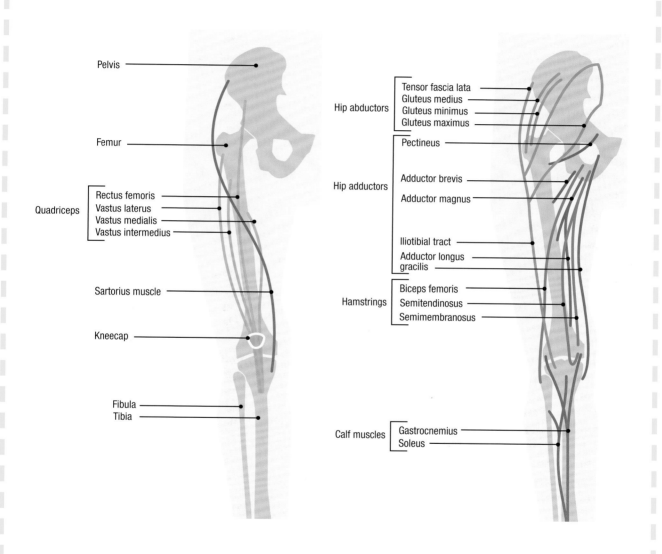

Pelvis

Femur

Quadriceps
Rectus femoris
Vastus laterus
Vastus medialis
Vastus intermedius

Sartorius muscle

Kneecap

Fibula
Tibia

Hip abductors
Tensor fascia lata
Gluteus medius
Gluteus minimus
Gluteus maximus

Pectineus

Hip adductors
Adductor brevis
Adductor magnus

Iliotibial tract
Adductor longus
gracilis

Hamstrings
Biceps femoris
Semitendinosus
Semimembranosus

Calf muscles
Gastrocnemius
Soleus

## Ankle injuries

Sprained and broken ankles are also common injuries that occur when playing roller derby. Ankle injuries occur very commonly in any sport that involves running, jumping, quick changes of direction or twisting and turning the ankle joint excessively. There are many opportunities for injury to the ankle because the ankle is a very complex structure made up of many ligaments, muscles, tendons and bones.

### What is a sprained ankle?

A sprained ankle is the stretching or tearing of the ligaments of the ankle joint. There are several different ligaments that keep the ankle joint stable. Those most prone to injury are the ligaments that stop the ankle rolling forward and outward which are the anterior talofibular ligament, the posterior talofibular ligament and the calcaneofibular ligament.

There are different degrees of injuries to these ligaments. A first-degree sprain means a minor stretching of the ligaments. This incurs mild pain, joint stiffness and swelling, but little loss of joint stability. A second-degree sprain will incur increased swelling and pain and moderate loss of stability. A third-degree sprain incurs severe pain and swelling and increased loss of stability. Sometimes, in the case of third-degree sprains, the localised pain will disappear soon after the injury occurs if the nerve endings have been severed, causing a lack of feeling at the injury state. In most cases, bruising will also occur depending on the severity of the injury. In the case of more serious ankle injuries, damage can also occur to the tendons that attach the muscles to the bones in the ankle, or even fractures to the bones in the ankle.

### Causes of ankle injuries

- Lack of warming-up and stretching
- Previous history of ankle sprains
- Lack of conditioning or weakness in the muscles, tendons or ligaments in the ankles

### Preventing ankle injuries

The best way to prevent ankle injuries is to stretch and strengthen the muscles, ligaments and tendons in the ankles as much as possible. Increasing the strength of these muscles will enable the body to better resist strains and injuries.

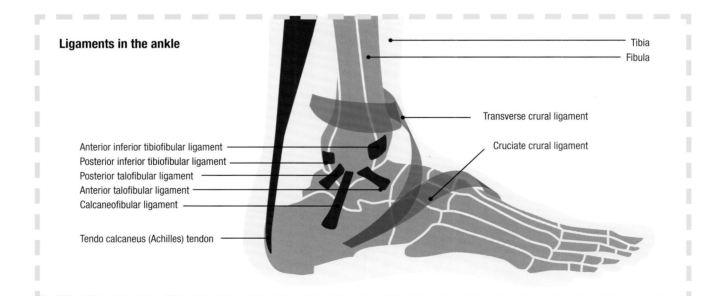

**Ligaments in the ankle**

Tibia
Fibula
Transverse crural ligament
Cruciate crural ligament
Anterior inferior tibiofibular ligament
Posterior inferior tibiofibular ligament
Posterior talofibular ligament
Anterior talofibular ligament
Calcaneofibular ligament
Tendo calcaneus (Achilles) tendon

## Ankle strengthening exercises
### Ankle plantarflexion

Plantarflexion is the movement that increases the angle between the foot and the shin, as when the foot is pressing a pedal or pointing the toes.

To strengthen this part of the ankle and foot, start by standing with your feet flat on the floor, hip-width apart. Raise your heels off the ground so you are standing on your tiptoes. Remain on your toes for six seconds before slowly returning to a standing position. This can be done from standing, or with the hands placed on a table or chair in front of you to aid stability.

### Ankle dorsiflexion

Dorsiflexion is where the dorsal, or top part of the foot is moved towards the shin.

To strengthen this part of the ankle and foot, start by standing with your feet flat on the floor, hip-width apart. Rock back onto your heels, lifting your toes off the floor. Remain on your heels for six seconds before slowly returning to a standing position. This can be done from standing, or with the hands placed on a table or chair in front of you to aid stability.

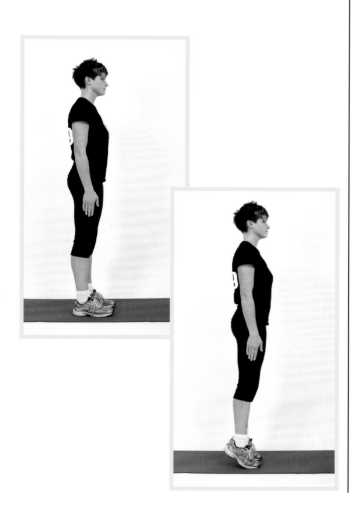

## Ankle inversion and eversion

To prevent ankle injuries and strengthen the weaker areas of the ankle and foot, slowly turn your left foot inward and hold this position for six seconds. This exercise can be done from sitting or standing, but hold the foot straight out in front of you with the foot off the ground. Now slowly turn your foot outward and hold for another six seconds. Then repeat with the other foot.

## Ankle alphabet

This exercise will help to strengthen all the muscles in the ankle. Hold the foot straight out in front of you with the foot off the ground. Write out the entire alphabet in the air with one foot, then repeat with the other foot.

## Looking after your back

Skating puts a lot of pressure on the lower back, especially if you aren't used to it. Skating in derby position for long periods often leaves new skaters feeling pain in the lower back. This can be combated by strengthening the muscles in the back and the core. Having a strong core will help support your spine when skating so any core exercises you do will therefore increase your body's ability to cope with strain it is placed under when playing roller derby.

## Lower back strengthening exercises

### Back hyperextensions

Start lying face down on an exercise mat with your arms outstretched in front of you. Raise your arm and head with the opposite leg and hold for three seconds. Keep looking down at the floor to avoid putting pressure on the neck. Lower your arm, leg and head at the same time and return to the starting position. Repeat the exercise with the opposite arm and leg for as many repetitions as required for your workout.

### Dorsal raise

Start lying face down on an exercise mat with your arms stretched out in front of you. With your arms resting by your temples, raise your arms and chest off the floor and hold for two to three seconds. Keep your feet on the floor to avoid putting too much pressure on the lower back. Lower your arms, chest and head back down to the starting position and repeat for as many reps as desired.

   For a more intense version of this exercise, the legs can also be lifted off the floor at the same time as the arms, chest and head.

# RECOVERING FROM INJURIES

If you do get injured, it is advisable to seek medical help from a doctor familiar with sports medicine so that an effective treatment and recovery programme can be established, allowing you to return to training as quickly and safely as possible. Every person and injury is unique so your doctor and/or physiotherapist will be able to help find the right treatment for you.

## SKATER PROFILE *KIT KAT POWER, LONDON ROCKIN' ROLLERS, LONDON, UK.*

**How has playing roller derby affected your overall health and fitness?**
I am stronger now: my legs are strong from skating and cycling so I'm trying to build up my abs and upper body strength.

**Have you ever sustained any injuries playing roller derby?**
I broke my ankle (the tibia and fibula)! I had a cast and was on crutches for seven long weeks. They were, probably, the longest weeks of my life. You can't do anything when you are on crutches. Well, you can build up your upper body, but to get around, walk the dog – everything is a challenge. I did it though.

**What did you do to aid your recovery and get back to training?**
I am so keen to get back to training 100 per cent but I need to allow my muscles to get back to where they were before. It's all about building up the rest around it, and doing lots of exercises focused on rebuilding the leg and foot. I do a lot of cycling, walking and short runs – and skate of course.

I have been really careful about not overdoing it, and am still very careful when I skate. I only just got the go-ahead from my physiotherapist, and I still have to take it easy. I am also working with a speed coach who has made a programme for me including all the activities I do every day such as cycling, running, walking and walking the dog. Next week we are going skating for a first practice session too. He's really good. Stretching is key, and upping the balance is too.

**What would you recommend doing as a skater to prevent injuries?**
Stretch, learn how to fall soft, don't slam down on your knees, or on any body part for that matter. Build yourself up slowly but surely. I have seen quite a few new girls starting and from being super scared they have gone to super confident, perhaps a bit overconfident, and then suddenly injured themselves. You have to ease yourself into it – especially if you are not used to doing any sports. Getting proper protective gear is also important.

# Nutrition

# NUTRITION FOR ROLLER DERBY

Diet is a very personal and subjective part of anyone's lifestyle. A lot of it comes down to personal tastes and habits, not to mention cultural differences and other personal lifestyle choices. The physical needs of every person are also very different depending on their height, weight, body composition, age and level of activity. I'm not here to tell anyone what they should and shouldn't do, but I will outline a few relevant nutritional facts for athletes, and you should take from them what you find most helpful.

It almost goes without saying that eating well will help anyone to feel good, especially those playing a very physically demanding sport such as roller derby. However, eating healthily and making sure your body has the right foods to use as fuel and for recovery doesn't have to be difficult. In this chapter, I will bring your attention to a few key points about nutrition to bear in mind as an athlete playing roller derby.

A little bit of planning goes a long way when it comes to what you eat before, during and after exercise. Good nutritional practices have been proven to increase energy and endurance, reduce fatigue, promote repair and recovery, reduce the risk of overtraining, maximise your fitness gains and support any training programme.

## Good nutrition practices

As a general rule, the best way to eat is to try to maintain an even blood sugar level as far as possible throughout each day so that your body doesn't experience sugar highs and crashes. This is the best way to ensure that you have the energy to do the training you want to do and benefit from it.

The best way to do this is to make sure your meals are composed of one-third lean protein and two-thirds complex carbohydrates. Lean proteins include lean meat, fish, eggs, pulses, nuts and seeds. Complex carbohydrates include whole grains, fruit and vegetables. This kind of balanced meal is much more likely to keep you full and your blood sugar even for longer so you don't experience a 'brain-starved-of-glucose' crash that makes you feel tired

and want to eat whatever is in your path. This rule is particularly important when it comes to breakfast, as this meal will dictate your blood sugar level for the rest of the day. Having small snacks of the same balance also helps to maintain blood sugar levels so having something to eat every three hours will also help to keep your energy levels up.

Chicken soup with lots of fresh vegetables is a good example of a balanced meal: one-third lean protein to two thirds complex carbohydrates.

# SKATER PROFILE *KRISSY KRASH, LA DERBY DOLLS, LOS ANGELES, USA*

**How long have you been playing roller derby?**
I started playing derby in May 2006.

**Did you skate before you started playing roller derby?**
I hadn't put on skates in 10 years when I went to my first practice.

**Did you play any other sports before you started playing roller derby?**
I played soccer for about 14 years. I was a goalkeeper and I think it has helped a lot with timing my hits in roller derby. I have also snowboarded since I was little. In college I boxed in a bar for a while. It was pretty fun.

**How has playing roller derby affected your overall health and fitness?**
I have always liked having something to train for so when I joined derby it was another new challenge and reason to work out harder.

**How often do you practise on skates?**
I am on skates two to three days a week.

**What other off-skates training do you do and how often?**
I train off skates four to six days a week. I work with a trainer on agility and strength. A few days a week I run or do interval sprints.

**Which other sports support roller derby?**
I think any kind of sport or exercise will help with overall fitness, but it's important to train for your sport specifically.

**What type of training has helped you to improve most as a skater?**
Plyometrics, agility ladders and long steady distance skating.

**What advice would you give to new skaters about training for roller derby?**
Run your own race. Work on being a little better every day and just know that like anything else mastery comes with practice.

**Are there any particular diet/nutrition practices that you follow to support your training?**
I make sure I eat enough protein to support my lean body mass. I take supplements to ensure I get my recommended amount of vitamins and minerals. I also keep a close on eye on post-workout recovery and hydration.

**How has your diet changed since you started roller derby?**
After skating for several years, I realised how important nutrition was to athletes, and started Derbalife, a nutrition programme aimed specifically at roller derby players. We do nutrition education, customised nutrition programmes and supplementation, as well as personal health coaching for skaters all over the world.

**What nutrition advice would you give to skaters new to the sport?**
Read up and educate yourself. Find out how much protein you need, eat small healthy meals throughout the day, and add supplement to ensure you get the right amounts of vitamins and minerals.

# SKATER PROFILE *ANAIS NINJA, GOTHAM GIRLS ROLLER DERBY, NEW YORK, USA*

**How long have you been playing roller derby?**
Three years – going into my fourth season.

**Did you play any other sports before roller derby?**
I was an awkward art nerd in school, so no, nothing like that in high school (I was pretty antisocial and angry). When I met my husband, he got me into kickboxing and boxing and oddly enough, I picked it up pretty fast and enjoyed it. I did that about two years before getting into derby. I realised I really like hitting things.

**How has playing roller derby affected your overall health and fitness?**
It's been a great influence to my exercise and eating habits. I take my other gym activities and sports a lot more seriously now because it helps my performance in derby and I feel overall just better physically – which extends to feeling better mentally. I used to smoke before starting sports and drink a lot and not care about my diet and I have done a 180. I'm a bit of a food Nazi when training.

**How often do you practise on skates?**
Three times a week.

**Which other sports support roller derby?**
From what I've seen, many of the girls with a soccer and/or hockey background do really great. Of course figure skating and speed skating are great too. This kills me because the one sport I wanted to do as a kid was figure skating but my parents wouldn't let me. Thanks mom and dad – I could've had a better start! (OK, just kidding – I'm really over it) From my (recent) background, I find martial arts very helpful in strengthening muscles not used in derby and with the mental part of the game and discipline.

**What type of training has helped improve most as a skater?**
Cardio and strength training! I'm a smaller skater so it's been important for me to remain strong while hit so I can maintain balance and not be literally thrown from the jam. Cardio is more obvious and super important so you can skate, get hit, hit others, etc constantly without winding. You have to be able to stay in the game and cardio gives you endurance. When you get knocked down, you have to jump right back up and pretend nothing happened.

**What advice would you give to new skaters about fitness/training for roller derby?**
Cross training is really important to be balanced. Just skating works out only certain muscles, leaving others weaker and this can lead to injury. Many girls neglect their upper body which can lead to awful injuries like separated shoulders and rotator cuff problems.

# HOW DOES FOOD PRODUCE ENERGY?

All food and drink is broken down to release energy one way or another, however different foods contain various macronutrients that do this in different ways. All foods are made up of different amounts of carbohydrates, proteins and fats and each of these macronutrients produce different amounts of energy. All foods contain a mixture of these nutrients and the amount of energy that can be released from each type of food depends on how much of each of these nutrients it contains.

## How does the body produce ATP?

Energy is produced in the body from the breakdown of carbohydrate, protein, fat and alcohol. These are broken down to produce a molecule called adenosine triphosphate, or ATP. This is a compound made up of adenosine and three groups of phosphate. Energy is stored in small amounts in every cell in the body in the form of ATP. Energy is produced in the splitting of the chemical bond between one of these phosphate groups and the adenosine. When ATP loses one of its phosphate groups it becomes adenosine diphosphate or ADP and is then converted into ATP again. This happens as a continuous cycle in which ATP is converted into ADP and then becomes ATP again. When ATP becomes ADP, energy is released. Some of this energy is used to carry out work and the rest is given off as heat. This is why you feel warm when exercising.

The different macronutrients in food are broken down to produce ATP. Energy is stored in the body in the form of ATP.

The body stores small amounts of ATP which is only enough to maintain the body at rest. When you are exercising, the amount of energy needed by the body is increased which means that more ATP must be produced in order for the body to be able to continue exercising. More fuel must be broken down to enable the body to produce more ATP. The body breaks down glucose that is found in the blood or in glycogen that is stored in your muscles and/or fat in order to do this.There are three main systems used by the body to produce ATP:

- The ATP-PC system
- The aerobic system
- The anaerobic glycolytic system

### The ATP-PC system

This system is used to generate energy to fuel short bursts of exercise lasting up to 10 seconds that require maximum strength and speed. PC is phosphocreatine which is a compound made up of the protein creatine linked to a phosphate molecule. PC breaks down into creatine and phosphate in order to regenerate ATP rapidly. The ATP-PC system can release energy very quickly but only for very short bursts, after this the body will rely on other systems to produce the energy it needs.

### The anaerobic glycolytic system

This system produces fuel for sudden, large demands for energy – usually high intensity exercise lasting for periods of up to 90 seconds. Muscle glycogen is rapidly broken down into glucose in the absence of oxygen to form ATP and lactic acid so that energy is available immediately. However, it is a very inefficient system as the quantity of ATP produced by each glucose molecule is much less than that produced by the aerobic system. When the body produces energy using the anaerobic glycolytic system, muscle glycogen stores become depleted very quickly and lactic acid builds up, which eventually leads to muscle fatigue.

### The aerobic system

This system is used to produce energy for longer periods of exercise at a slower rate than the anaerobic or ATP-PC systems. The aerobic system generates energy through the breakdown of carbohydrates and fat in the presence of oxygen. Glucose derived from stored muscle glycogen is converted into ATP as oxygen is transported to the muscles. However, after the first hour of exercise, muscle glycogen will start to run low and then the body will also use increasing amounts of fat as fuel. Fat has the capacity to produce large amounts of energy but it can only be broken down using the aerobic system. This system produces much larger amounts of ATP over a longer period of time and is the most efficient system of producing energy for exercise.

Some sources recommend eating a high GI snack such as dried fruit an hour before training to top up glycogen stores so you have enough readily available energy.

# HOW IS ENERGY PRODUCED FOR EXERCISE?

Athletes of almost all sports use all three energy systems to a greater or lesser extent. The different systems for producing energy work together, not independently, so when the aerobic and anaerobic systems work together to produce energy it is not a question of which system the body is using at a given time but which system is dominating energy production.

Athletes playing roller derby use a combination of the anaerobic glycolytic and the aerobic systems to produce energy. Therefore, stored muscle glycogen and some fat are the main sources of fuel. In a bout consisting of two half-hour periods made up of short jams of up to two minutes, the anaerobic glycolytic system is likely to be dominant because the body requires fuel for short periods of high intensity. However, in a two-hour training session consisting of drills and endurance, the aerobic system is likely to be a more dominant source of energy production.

The source of fuel for energy production depends largely on the intensity and duration of exercise. The average person has enough stored muscle glycogen to fuel 90–180 minutes of endurance exercise depending on the intensity of the exercise. During high-intensity, mainly anaerobic activities, muscle glycogen stores can become depleted within 30–45 minutes.

## Level of fitness

The fitness level can have a great effect on the way the body produces fuel for exercise. As the body becomes fitter as a result of aerobic training, it becomes more efficient at breaking down fat into fatty acids, which are transported to the muscle cells and can be used as fuel. This means that the fitter you are, the less reliant your body will be on using stored muscle glycogen. If your body is more efficient at breaking down fat, this means you will be able to exercise for longer because using fat as fuel will enable you to spare stored muscle glycogen, meaning that it will take longer for muscle glycogen to become depleted and the muscles to become fatigued.

## Energy sources for exercise

The higher the intensity of exercise, the more your body will rely on carbohydrates stored as muscle glycogen. For moderate-intensity exercise 50–70 per cent of maximum aerobic capacity, stored muscle glycogen supplies half your energy, and for high-intensity exercise of over 70 per cent, stored muscle glycogen provides three-quarters of your energy. The majority of energy used in any type of anaerobic exercise comes from stored muscle glycogen, and for aerobic exercise it comes from a mixture of carbohydrates stored as glycogen and fat. However, when glycogen stores become depleted, muscle proteins also start to break down to make amino acids available for energy production.

## Roller derby burns calories

When doing any exercise, the body is required to produce energy faster than when it is resting. When exercising, the muscles, heart and lungs are all working harder and more energy is required to do so.

Anyone playing roller derby will be burning a lot of calories and this is something to bear in mind when it comes to diet. Studies have shown that a person weighing 65kg/143lbs skating at 16kph/10mph can burn up to 600 calories per hour and people skating at 9.5kph/6mph can burn up to 350 calories per hour. Most leagues hold at least two two-hour practices every week, and this means that, in one league practice alone, you could be burning up to 1,000 calories – not to mention any additional cross-training or off-skates training you may be doing. Any athlete needs to eat enough of the right kinds of food to support the training they are doing on a daily basis.

# NUTRITION FOR ATHLETES

To gain the maximum exercise benefit from the food you eat it's necessary to eat a balance of different nutrients, adjusting types and quantities depending on the type of workout that you are doing.

## Carbohydrates

Carbohydrate is an important energy source for exercise. Carbohydrate is stored as glycogen in the liver and muscles. Roughly 400g (14oz) of glycogen can be stored in the muscles and 100g (3.5oz) in the liver but this must be replenished every day. Glycogen stored in the muscles is used to fuel physical activity, whereas glycogen stored in the liver is used to maintain steady blood sugar levels. When the blood glucose level is low, glycogen stored in the liver is broken down to release glucose into the bloodstream.

Because carbohydrate is the main source of energy for most exercise, the more active you are, the more carbohydrate your body needs. Glycogen storage capacity is proportional to muscle mass and body weight, as well as how much training you do. The recommended daily intakes are:

- 5–7g (0.2–0.25oz) per kg (2.2lb) of body weight for moderate duration/low intensity daily training
- 7–10g (0.25–0.35oz) per kg (2.2lb) of body weight for moderate–heavy endurance training
- 10g+ (0.35oz) per kg (2.2lb) of body weight for those training more than four hours a day

All exercising athletes need to consume carbohydrate as part of a balanced diet. There is a lot of evidence to suggest that a low-carbohydrate diet will result in low muscle and liver glycogen stores, causing lower ability to sustain high-intensity exercise for longer than an hour. The amount of glycogen stored in your muscles and liver has a direct effect on performance. When glycogen stores are depleted, the body will increasingly rely on fat as fuel, but this is not a recommended method for losing fat as lean muscle tissue will be broken down as well, as the body starts to break down muscle protein when glycogen stores are depleted.

## Carbohydrates and the glycaemic index

There are, however, different types of carbohydrates and these have different effects on the body. The glycaemic index (GI) is a system of ranking carbohydrates based on the immediate effect they have on blood sugar levels. Carbohydrates with a high GI produce a rapid rise in blood sugar and carbohydrates with a low GI produce a slow rise in blood sugar. In the glycaemic index, foods are given a ranking from 0 to 100 based on their immediate

Pasta is a low GI carbohydrate food. It is important for athletes to eat carbohydrates before training as your glycogen levels will affect your performance.

# SKATER PROFILE *RAW HEIDI*

**How long have you been playing roller derby?**
I have been playing for four years.

**Did you skate before you started roller derby?**
I did a lot of street skating as a teenager on my blades as well as some ramps.

**Did you play any other sports before you started playing roller derby?**
I was never a sporty child or teenager, I was never inspired to play any team or solo sports as I thought them slightly pointless. That's all changed now.

**How has roller derby affected your overall health and fitness?**
I have become progressively fitter and stronger and in 2011 I was the fittest I have ever been in my life by a long stretch.

**How often do you practise on skates?**
Three or four times a week.

**What other off-skates training do you do and how often?**
I do a variety of calisthenics every weekday morning, I play squash and have picked up and dropped various exercise regimes over the past few years. I have never stuck at anything long enough to get good at it except roller derby.

**Which other sports support roller derby?**
I can't think of a sport that doesn't have something that can be taken from it to improve your game. Anything that involves explosive movement, core strength, balance, cardiovascular fitness, strength conditioning will support a roller derby player's training. I am looking into taking up yoga this year.

**What type of training has helped you to improve most as a skater?**
My biggest upward spike in physical ability happened when I started to work seriously on my core. It's been an intrinsic part of all my training ever since. It doesn't matter how big or small or fierce you are – if you hit someone with a solid core they aren't going anywhere.

**What advice would you give to new skaters about training for roller derby?**
Take it at your own pace but work initially on building up your ankle, thigh and core strength to prevent injury. On the track footwork and agility are key and must not be underestimated: you need to really get to know your skates and how you move on them, then challenge yourself to move in unusual ways once you've mastered the basics. The only person you should be in competition with is yourself: only you can push your game and performance to the next level.

**Are there any nutritional practices you follow to support your training?**
On training days I will make sure I have had enough complex carbohydrates to ensure I have the energy I need for what I want to achieve at practice. I have a protein shake after any kind of intensive training to replenish and help build lean muscle. Before games and during tournaments I try to eat only what I know I need (usually complex carbs and protein) and make sure I am totally hydrated.

**How has your diet changed since you started roller derby?**

I never thought much about my diet beyond what tasted good, now I think a lot about how much of each food group I am taking on in relation to what I want my body to do for me. I love food and eating to train doesn't dominate my life, but I still think about it every day. As a result I am skinnier than I have been for years but still around the same weight as when I started training, which is great as it means my body fat has become muscle.

Oats and other wholegrain cereals are low GI foods. Oats are perfect for an athlete's diet as they also contain protein.

effect on blood sugar levels; the higher the rating, the faster the rise in blood sugar. It may be more helpful to think of foods in groups of high GI (71–100), medium GI (56–70) and low GI (0–55). As a general rule, refined starchy foods such as potatoes, white rice and white bread and sugary foods such as soft drinks have a high GI and less refined starchy foods such as porridge, lentils, beans, wholegrain cereal, fruit and dairy products have a lower GI. To find the GI for a particular food, you can refer to the website www.glycemicindex.com which has up-to-date information about the GI values of many different kinds of foods.

The GI of a food is determined by the size of the particles in the food, the type of starch present in the food, the sugar content of the food and the amount of fibre that the food contains. The presence of fibre in a food slows down the digestion, producing a lower rise in blood sugar. Eating any carbohydrate foods with protein or fat will lower the GI because both protein and fat slow down the digestion of food, producing a lower rise in blood sugar.

A low GI diet is recommended for athletes because the key to the most efficient glycogen refuelling is to maintain steady levels of blood glucose and insulin. When high GI foods are consumed, the body produces high levels of insulin, turning the excess glucose into fat cells. Highs of blood glucose are also followed by lows that produce sugar cravings due to blood glucose fluctuations.

A low GI diet consists of carbohydrate foods with a low GI combined with lean protein foods and healthy fats. This includes lots of fresh fruit and vegetables, wholemeal and wholegrain breads, low GI carbohydrates such as noodles, oats, pasta, basmati rice, bulgur wheat and quinoa, all types of beans and lentils, nuts and seeds, low GI cereals including oat and rye cereals and porridge, lean meat, fish, tofu and eggs, soya and low-fat dairy products.

It is not only the type of food that produces a rapid rise in blood glucose. The quantity of food that you eat also affects the level of glucose in your bloodstream. Eating a small quantity of a high GI carbohydrate and eating a large quantity of a low GI food will both result in a surge in blood glucose. It is therefore advisable to eat little and often and avoid overloading on carbohydrates, making sure you have a balance of carbohydrate, protein and healthy fat in every meal.

## Protein

Proteins make up part of the structure of every cell and tissue in the body including muscle tissue, tendons, internal organs, skin, hair and nails. Protein is used for growth and repair of cells and forming new tissue in the body, as well as making enzymes, hormones and antibodies. Athletes need to consume more protein than those who are inactive because their bodies need to recover from the muscle breakdown that occurs during and after exercise and also build new muscle.

Fish is a great source of lean protein for athletes. Salmon and other oily fish also contain Omega-3 fatty acids which are an important part of an athlete's diet

The recommended intake of protein is between 1.2 and 1.7g (0.04–0.06oz) per kg (2.2lb) of body weight for athletes, depending on the level and intensity of activity, and 0.75g (0.03oz) per kg (2.2lb) of body weight for a sedentary person.

During digestion, proteins are broken down into amino acids. There are 20 amino acids in total, which make up thousands of kinds of protein in different combinations. Twelve of the amino acids can be made in the body from other amino acids, carbohydrate and nitrogen. The other eight amino acids that the body needs must be provided by diet, as they cannot be made in the body. Essential amino acids are isoleucine, leucine, lysine, methionine, phenylalanine, threonine, tryptophan and valine.

Meat, fish, dairy and soya products contain all eight amino acids but proteins that come from plants, such as nuts, seeds and pulses don't contain all eight, so they need to be combined and eaten together in order for the body to get all the amino acids it requires.

Legumes, lentils, peas, seeds, nuts, greens, fruit, lean meat or fish, tofu, soya and low-fat dairy products are all sources of lean protein. However, meat has a higher protein content per serving.

## Fats

Some fat is essential to the diet in order to maintain healthy joints and organs. Fats also make up part of the brain tissue, cell membranes and bone marrow. Fats in food are broken down into fatty acids and are used as a long-term store of energy, as well as providing fat-soluble vitamins A, D and E. Fat is also an important energy source for exercise.

It is recommended that between 20 and 33 per cent of the calories in your diet should come from fat. However, there are different types of fats, some of which are healthier than others. 'Bad' fats are saturated fats and trans-fats that are found in animal products and palm oil. These have no health benefits and it is recommended that less than 10 per cent of calories you consume should come from

A balanced diet containing plenty of fresh fruit and vegetables should provide an athlete with all the necessary vitamins and minerals to suit the body's needs.

these kinds of fats. These types of fats can increase cholesterol and the risk of heart disease. 'Good' fats are unsaturated fats that include monounsaturates and polyunsaturates found in nuts, seeds, fish, olives, avocados, and the oils that come from these sources. Monounsaturated fats lower the levels of harmful cholesterol, also known as low-density lipoprotein, while increasing the levels of good cholesterol, or high-density lipoprotein. Polyunsaturated fats include omega-3 and omega-6 fatty acids.

Omega-3 fatty acids are important for athletes because they help recovery, increase the delivery of oxygen to the muscles and help maintain healthy joints by reducing stiffness and inflammation. They also reduce recovery time from injuries. Omega-3 fats include eicosapentaenoic acid and docosahexaenoic acid that are found only in oily fish. These can also be formed by the body from alpha-linoleic acid which can be found in linseeds, pumpkin seeds, walnuts, rapeseed oil and leafy green vegetables such as spinach and kale. Omega-3 fatty acids reduce the viscosity of the blood so help prevent stroke and heart disease. They are also help the proper

functioning of the brain. Omega-6 fatty acids are important for the functioning of cell membranes and healthy skin. Omega-6 fatty acids include linoleic acid, gamma-linoleic acid and docosapentaenoic acid, and are contained in a wider variety of foods than omega-3 fatty acids because they are present in vegetable oils (and polyunsaturated margarine).

## Fibre

Fibre is essential for maintaining a healthy digestive system – something that is important for everyone, especially athletes. Fibre changes the glycaemic effect of a meal because it slows down the digestion of carbohydrate, meaning a slower rise in blood glucose. By slowing down the time it takes your body to process foods, fibre also maximises the amount of nutrients the body can absorb throughout the digestion process. Foods with high fibre content include beans, lentils, oats, rye, fruit and vegetables. Including foods high in fibre to your nutritional intake can help you to feel full longer, absorb more nutrients and allow healthy bowel function.

Supplements can be taken to ensure that you are getting all the vitamins and minerals your body needs. Cod liver oil tablets provide extra omega-3 fatty acids to help maintain healthy joints.

## Vitamins and minerals

Vitamins are required for growth, health and overall physical well-being. Our bodies cannot produce vitamins so we need to consume them on a daily basis. Many vitamins are required for the functioning of the central nervous system, the immune system and the hormonal system.

Minerals are essential to certain structural and regulatory roles in the functioning of the body such as muscle contraction, nerve function, controlling fluid balance and the formation of red blood cells. Like vitamins, the body cannot produce minerals so these must be supplied by our diet.

A balanced diet containing plenty of fresh fruit and vegetables should provide all the necessary vitamins and minerals to meet the body's needs. However, as food-processing and intensive-farming practices have become more common, the nutritional content of many foods has deteriorated, making it harder to get enough vitamins and minerals. Lifestyle can also make eating a balanced diet more difficult, particularly for those who work long hours, train at irregular times and have to eat on the go.

Regular and intense exercise can also increase the need for vitamins and minerals used for tissue repair and growth, energy metabolism and red blood cell production, most importantly, vitamin E, vitamin C, B vitamins thiamine, riboflavin and niacin, vitamin B6, vitamin B5, folic acid, vitamin B12, calcium, potassium and iron. These vitamins and minerals are all fundamental to many processes in the body that are particularly necessary for exercising athletes so it is essential that athletes ensure they are getting enough of all of these vitamins and minerals from their diet.

A balanced diet is the best source of vitamins and minerals. However, supplements can be taken to ensure that you are getting the essential vitamins and minerals that your body needs every day. It is important to bear in mind that the body can only absorb a certain amount of each vitamin or mineral each day and any amount ingested above that will be excreted. Some vitamins can even be harmful if taken in very large quantities: vitamins A, D and B6 can be toxic in high doses of more than ten times the recommended daily intake.

### Immune system

Some athletes will find that periods of intense training leave them more susceptible to catching colds and other infections. Although it has been proven that moderate exercise boosts the immune system, it is thought that increased levels of cortisol and adrenaline in the body during periods of intense training can reduce immune cell production. Taking a multivitamin or a vitamin C supplement regularly will help boost your immune system and resistance to infections.

# SKATER PROFILE *RED N' ROLL, LONDON ROCKIN' ROLLERS, LONDON, UK*

**How long have you been playing roller derby?**
I've been playing for three years.

**Are there any particular nutrition practices you follow to support your training?**
I use the Derbalife nutrition plan to help me eat like an athlete. It's based around eating every two to three hours, and getting the correct amount of protein in your diet for what your fitness goals are, plus I get to drink yummy shakes for breakfast every day.

**How has your diet changed since you started roller derby?**
Before I played roller derby, I would try to eat healthily, but often cost and convenience took over. Nowadays I always try to eat fresh. What I did was to just change one thing at a time such as first incorporating more fruit, then more vegetables, then thinking about protein for every meal and about how often I ate. If you did it all at once you would never keep it up because it has such a big effect on your life.

**What advice about diet would you give to skaters who are new to the sport?**
Just try and think about what you put into your bodies before you train. If you feed your body with crap, then you won't have the energy to keep playing. But if you fuel yourself with some complex carbs and lean protein then you will get much more out of your sessions because you will be able to push yourself just that little bit further.

**How has playing roller derby affected your overall health and fitness?**
I am the fittest I have ever been. When I played netball I did it for fun so I never cross-trained, and I would often be tired after an hour-long match. Because roller derby means so much to me, I put in the extra effort to make myself stronger and to keep my endurance up. Now I can play two hour-long bouts in a row. To me that's like I've doubled my energy output, and it makes me smile.

**How often do you practise on skates?**
We train three times a week, for two, two-hour sessions during the week, but on Sundays I can be on skates for six hours at times when I am playing and coaching.

**What other off-skates training do you do and how often?**
I cycle 5 miles every day to commute to work and back. On training days I carry my kit bag on my back and I'll cycle from work to training (about 20 minutes) then home again afterwards (about 35 minutes). On Sundays I cycle up to an hour to get to training, then cycle home again after practice. Often I will also jump on my bike trainer at home and do my own version of spinning class or tabata intervals, or I will do some plyometrics.

**What type of training has helped you to improve most as a skater?**
When I was first learning how to skate, my cycling definitely gave me the edge over other skaters at my level. I saw my endurance shoot right up, and I could push myself harder for longer because of it.

**What advice would you give to new skaters about training for roller derby?**
I would say that if you want to get better quickly you have to cross-train in another sport as soon as possible. Whether it is swimming, cycling, jogging or whatever, it doesn't matter, but you will benefit fast.

# EATING AND EXERCISING

What you eat before training, the time at which you eat, and how much you eat all have a noticeable effect on your performance, strength and endurance during exercise. Ideally, you should try to eat two to four hours before exercise to give your body a chance to digest the food and replenish muscle glycogen levels so you don't feel hungry, but don't feel too full either.

Many sources advise eating a low GI meal containing 2.5g (0.1oz) of carbohydrate per kg (2.2lb) of body weight, for example pasta with tomato sauce, vegetables and cheese, a tuna sandwich with salad or muesli with milk and fruit.

It is important to eat carbohydrates before exercise, as it is your glycogen levels that will most affect your performance. Eating protein is more important after exercise as protein predominantly builds and repairs, not fuels muscle.

Some sources also suggest that eating high GI/simple carbohydrate snack such as bananas, dried figs, dates and pineapple one to two hours before training will top up glycogen stores so you will have more readily available fuel for energy.

## Eating during training

Most roller derby training sessions last at least two hours and a bout lasts for two periods of thirty minutes each. If you are exercising for more than an hour at a time, you should eat some carbohydrate while you are exercising in order to delay fatigue and continue exercising when muscle glycogen stores are depleted and blood sugar starts getting low.

When exercising for longer than one hour, you should try to consume 30–60g (1–2oz) of carbohydrates per hour. For the best effects, try to consume some carbohydrates before you experience fatigue, within the first 30 minutes of exercise.

Anything you eat during exercise needs to be something that your body can easily absorb. Drinks that contain carbohydrates are ideal, as they will help you stay hydrated as well as providing some fuel for your muscles.

Replacing salt, trace minerals, potassium and electrolytes while training is also a good idea. Electrolytes are mineral salts including sodium, chloride, potassium and magnesium that are present in the body's fluids. They help to regulate the fluid balance in the body. Some sports drinks and coconut water contain electrolytes, while a litre (34fl oz) of diluted apple juice with a quarter teaspoon of salt added does a similar job.

## Eating after training

What you eat in the hours after exercise is very important, as this is what your body uses to recover and replenish after exertion.

The length of time it will take your body to refuel depends on how depleted your glycogen stores are after training, your overall fitness level, the extent of muscle damage and the food that you eat in order to recover. The fitter you are, the more efficient your body becomes at replenishing glycogen stores. A person who is fitter will be able to recover more quickly than someone less fit eating the same food.

The extent to which glycogen stores are depleted depends on the intensity of exercise. Roller derby uses a lot of fast, explosive movements which means that glycogen stores will be a lot more depleted after playing roller derby than doing a less intense form of exercise such as jogging. The duration of exercise also affects how much glycogen stores are depleted – the longer you spend exercising, the more depleted your glycogen stores will be.

It is best to eat as soon as possible after training as the body is more efficient at storing glycogen during the two hours immediately after exercise than

It is best to eat as soon as possible after training to aid recovery and replenishing of glycogen stores. A protein shake or a smoothie made with bananas and yoghurt is a perfect post-training snack.

at any other time. During the subsequent four hours, glycogen storage still occurs faster than normal but the rate slows dow. Eating carbohydrate during this time is most important for recovery.

The more carbohydrate you eat after exercise, the more quickly you will be able to replenish your glycogen stores. It is also very important to eat protein after exercise as many different studies have concluded that combining protein with carbohydrate is more effective for promoting glycogen recovery than eating carbohydrate alone. This is because eating protein and carbohydrate together stimulates the production of insulin, which speeds up the muscles' uptake of amino acids and glucose from the bloodstream. Protein is essential for recovery as it is necessary for muscle repair and growth.

A post-workout meal should include protein and carbohydrate in a ratio of 1:4. Carbohydrate should be the foundation of your meal to replenish glycogen stores, with protein to aid recovery. Good snacks to eat in the two hours after exercise include a protein shake, a sandwich filled with lean protein such as tuna, chicken, cottage cheese or egg. A smoothie made with fresh fruit and yoghurt, wholegrain cereal with milk, or a baked potato with a lean protein filling such as tuna, cottage cheese or beans.

## Hydration

When you play roller derby or do any other sort of hard exercise you lose fluid through sweating. This is because when you exercise, your body temperature rises so you sweat in order to cool the body down and regulate body temperature. If this fluid is not replaced as you are exercising you can get dehydrated, which will have an adverse effect on your physical performance as you will feel fatigued more quickly and exercising will feel much harder.

The amount of fluid you lose through sweating depends on how hard and how long you are exercising for and will vary from person to person under different temperature conditions. The harder and longer you exercise and the hotter the conditions, the more fluid you will lose. Fluid loss through sweating also depends on body size and fitness level.

To prevent dehydration during training, always make sure you are well hydrated before exercise, especially in hot or humid weather. Drinking 400–600ml (13–20fl oz) of water in the two hours before exercise is recommended in order to ensure that you are fully hydrated when you begin training. It is also recommended that you replace at least 80 per cent of the fluid you lose through sweating during training. During intense training and hot temperature conditions you could be losing more than 1 litre (34fl oz) of water per hour and this needs to be replaced in order to prevent dehydration. It is also important to drink plenty of water after exercise in order to replace fluid lost during training. Many different sources recommend 1.5–2 litres (50–70fl oz) of water every day as the optimum amount to stay hydrated.

# NUTRITION FOR VEGETARIAN AND VEGAN ATHLETES

Many athletes choose a vegetarian or vegan diet for many different reasons. Many people think that a vegetarian or vegan diet cannot fulfil an athlete's nutritional requirements, but will some careful planning, there is no reason why a vegan or vegetarian athlete cannot get the nutrients they need.

In fact, many surveys have found that people eating a plant-based diet have a healthier diet than meat-eaters because they have higher intakes of fruit and vegetables, fibre, antioxidants and phytonutrients and lower intakes of saturated fat and cholesterol than those eating meat and other animal products.

In general, a vegan or vegetarian diet is lower in protein than a non-vegetarian diet, so vegetarian and vegan athletes need to take extra care that they consume a variety of protein-rich foods in order to meet their dietary needs.

Most foods contain at least some protein, so it is not difficult for vegan and vegetarian athletes to consume enough protein. It is the balance of consuming the right sources of protein to ensure that you are getting all eight essential amino acids that takes a bit more planning and consideration.

Single-plant foods do not contain enough of all the essential amino acids in the right proportions. For example, grains are short of lysine and pulses are short of methionine. However, mixing different types of plant foods together means that it is quite easy to achieve a high-quality protein intake containing all the essential amino acids your body

Athletes who don't eat red meat must be careful that they are consuming enough iron. Spinach is a great source of iron for vegan and vegetarian athletes.

Soya milk and other products are a great source of protein for vegetarian and vegan athletes.

Vegans must be careful that they ar eating proteins from a number of different types of food to ensure they consume all the essential amino acids the body needs. Protein complementing is an easy way to do this, for example, mixing nuts with wholegrains.

needs. This is known as protein complementing and can be achieved by combining any two or more of the following types of foods: pulses, including beans lentils and peas; grains, including bread, rice, oats, pasta and other cereals; quorn or soya products; nuts and seeds. Some examples of protein complementing include peanut butter on wholegrain toast, tofu with vegetables and rice or lentil soup with wholegrain bread.

Vegans and vegetarians also need to ensure that they consume enough omega-3 fatty acids. Omega -3 fatty acids include eicosapentaenoic acid and docosahexaenoic acid that are found only in oily fish. However, these can also be formed by the body from alpha-linoleic acid that can be found in linseeds, pumpkin seeds, walnuts, rapeseed oil and leafy green vegetables such as spinach and kale.

Athletes who do not eat red meat must make sure they consume enough iron from other sources. Iron is very important for athletes because it is essential for the formation of haemoglobin, which transports oxygen in the blood, and myoglobin, which transports oxygen in the muscle cells.

Vegan athletes in particular run the risk of a deficiency in vitamin B12. Vitamin B12 is involved in red blood cell and bone marrow production, as well as cell division and protein manufacture. Vitamin B12 can be found in foods such as Marmite and some cereals, or in fermented foods such as miso or tempeh.

# Glossary

**Assist** Motion administered by one player to help another player (usually the jammer) gain advantage. An assist can include pushing, pulling, redirecting or whipping another skater.

**Blocker** Defensive skater position. Blockers set up plays to help their jammer or block the opposing jammer.

**Blocking zone** Part of the body with which it is permissible to hit another skater. Blocking must be done to a legal target zone. Legal blocking zones include the arms from the shoulder to above the elbow; the torso; the hips; the butt; and the mid- and upper thigh. Illegal blocking zones include elbows; forearms; hands; head; and any part of the leg below the mid-thigh.

**Bout** A roller derby game is referred to as a bout. A bout is usually broken up into two 30-minute halves, and those halves are broken up into jams of up to two minutes.

**Call off the jam** The lead jammer can call off or cancel the jam at any time.

**Crossover** Crossing one foot over the other when skating to aid acceleration.

**Cut track** Crossing the infield to rejoin the pack after you fall or are blocked out of bounds.

**Falling small** Trying to keep your body as small as possible when hitting the ground to prevent other skaters from tripping over you. If you do not fall small, you may incur a major penalty by tripping another player.

**Fresh meat** New skaters.

**Helmet panty** Helmet covers worn by the jammer and pivot to identify their positions.

**Hip check** A bump delivered using the hips while skating immediately next to the target.

**Hit** To block using full contact.

**Jammer** Scoring skater position designated by a star on her helmet. Her objective is to score one point per opposing blocker she laps.

**Jammer line** A starting line on the track, located behind the pivot line, from which the jammers depart on the referee's second whistle. Jammers may touch, but not cross, the line. If a jammer crosses the jammer line before the second whistle, it is designated a false start.

**Jumping the apex** In roller derby this term refers to jumping over the apex of the bend on the inside line of the track to get past someone who is holding the inside line.

**Juking** The juke is also known as a 'jab step' and is used in many other sports as well as roller derby. In roller derby jukes are short sharp steps that can be used by a skater to free oneself from their opposition by changing direction very quickly at the last moment.

**Lead jammer** The jammer who gets through the pack first and the only jammer who is able to call off a jam.

**Non-scoring pass** The jammer's first pass through the pack. During this pass, the jammer is eligible to obtain lead jammer status, but does not score any points.

**NSO** A non-skating official. The NSOs help with various referee duties during the bouts, including penalty tracking, timing the penalty box, keeping track of points and collecting data for later statistical analyses.

**Pack** The mass of blockers from both teams skating around the track together. Each jammer's goal is to get through the pack and score points.

**Penalty box** A designated area off the track where skaters who have committed fouls are sent to serve time.

**Pivot** A blocker designated by a stripe down the middle of her helmet cover and known as the pacesetter for the pack.

**Pivot line** The starting line for the pack that is in front of the jammer line. Only the pivot is permitted to start on the pivot line; all other blockers must be lined up behind her hips. The pack may cross the pivot line once the referee blows the first whistle to signal the start of the jam. If any skater crosses the line before the whistle, it is designated a false start.

**Ploughing** A plough is a type of stop used in roller derby that involves spreading your feet and angling one or both feet inwards so as to plough to a stop. Much like a 'snowplough' stop in skiing.

**Positional blocking** Using the body to obstruct another skater's path rather than forcefully hitting him or her.

**Power jam** A situation whereby one team's jammer has been sent to the penalty box, and thus only the team with a jammer on the track can score.

**Scoring pass** Any pass through the pack after the jammer's first pass (the non-scoring pass). At this time the jammer racks up points for each opponent she passes.

**Scrimmage** A practice game that isn't open to the public.

**Star pass** When the jammer passes her helmet panty to the pivot, who then takes over as jammer.

**Target zone** An area of the body that may be hit. Legal target zones include hands, arms, chest, abdomen, sides, hips, and the front and sides of the legs to the mid-thigh. Illegal target zones include the head, neck, back, butt, back of the thighs and any part of the leg below mid-thigh.

**Whip** An assisted move in which a skater extends her arm and whips her jammer around the track, propelling her with momentum.

**Zebra** Referees and NSOs are referred to as zebras because of their black-and-white uniforms.

# Further reading and resources

## Books

*Flat Track Fashion: The Roller Derby Look Book* by Ellen Parnavelas. A&C Black, 2011.

*Rollergirl: Totally True Tales from the Track* by Melissa Joulwan. Touchstone Books, 2007.

*Down and Derby* by Jennifer Barbee Alex Cohen. Soft Skull Press, 2011.

*No Mercy: Roller Derby Life on the Track* by Jules Doyle. Schiffer Publishing Ltd, 2011.

*Roller Derby: The History and All-Girl Revival of the Greatest Sport on Wheels* by Catherine Mabe. Spek Press, 2007.

*Roller Derby to Rollerjam (Tr)* by Keith Coppage. Squarebooks, 1999.

*Five Strides on the Banked Track: The Life and Times of the Roller Derby* by Frank Deford. Little Brown & Company, 1971.

*The Complete Guide to Stretching* by Christopher M. Norris. A&C Black, 2007.

*The Anatomy of Stretching: Your Illustrated Guide to Flexibility and Injury Rehabilitation* by Brad Walker. Lotus Publishing, 2011.

*Dynamic Stretching* by Mark Kovacs. Ulysees Press, 2009.

*Plyometrics for Athletes at All Levels*. Ulysees Press, 2006.

*Developing Agility and Quickness* (Sports Performance) by the National Strength and Conditioning Association. Human Kinetics, 2011.

*High-powered Plyometrics* by J.C. Radcliffe and R.C. Farentinos. Human Kinetics, 1999.

*The Complete Guide to Core Stability* by Matt Lawrence. A&C Black, 2007.

*Delavier s Core Training Anatomy* by Frederic Delavier and Michael Gundhill. Human Kinetics, 2011.

*You Are Your Own Gym: The Bible of Bodyweight Exercises* by Mark Lauren. Light of New Orleans Publishing, 2011.

*Principles and Practice of Resistance Training* by Michael Stone, Margaret Stone and William A. Sands. Human Kinetics, 2007.

*Fitness Trainers: Interval Training for Fitness* by Joseph T. Nitti and Kimberlie Nitti. Bloomsbury, 2002.

*The BMA Guide to Sport Injuries* by Dorling Kindersley, 2010.

*Sports Injuries: Their Prevention and Treatment* by Lars Peterson and Per Renstrom. Informa Healthcare, 2000.

*The Complete Guide to Sports Nutrition* (Complete Guides) by Anita Bean. A&C Black, 2009.

*Anita Bean s Sports Nutrition for Women: A Practical Guide for Active Women* by Anita Bean. A&C Black, 2010.

*Vegetarian Sports Nutrition* by Enette Larson Meyer. Human Kinetics, 2006.

*Vegan Bodybuilding & Fitness: The Complete Guide to Building Your Body on a Plant-Based Diet* by Robert Cheeke. Healthy Living Publications, 2011.

## Magazines

*Blood and Thunder Magazine*
http://www.bloodandthundermag.com/

*Five on Five*
http://fiveonfivemag.com/

*Fracture*
http://www.fracturemag.com/

*Inside Line*
http://www.insidelinemagazine.co.uk/

*Lead Jammer Magazine*
http://www.leadjammermag.com/

*Hit & Miss*
http://www.hitandmissmagazine.com.au/

## Suppliers
### Skates, pads and other kit

*Atom Wheels*
http://www.atomwheels.com/

*Bones Bearings*
http://www.bonesbearings.com/

*Billy s*
http://www.billys.co.uk/

*Cruz Skate Shop*
http://cruzskateshop.com/

*Emerald City Skates*
http://www.emeraldcityskates.com/

*Everglides*
http://www.everglides.co.uk/

*Fast Girl Skates*
http://www.fastgirlskates.com/

*Pro Designed*
http://www.prodesigned.com/

*Proline Skates*
http://www.prolineskates.com (UK)

*Pro-Tec*
http://www.pro-tec.net/

*Radar Wheels*
http://www.radarwheels.com/

*Riedell*
http://www.riedellskates.com/

*Rocky Mountain Skates*
http://www.shop.rockymountainskates.com/

*Roller Derby Depot*
http://www.rollerderbydepot.com/

*Roller Derby Shop*
http://www.rollerderbyshop.com/

*Roller Derby Virginia Beach*
http://www.rollerderbyvb.com/

*Rollergirl Skates*
http://www.rollergirlskates.com/

**RollerGirl.CA**
http://www.rollergirl.ca/

**Roller Guy Skates**
http://www.rollerguyskates.com/

**Sin City Skates**
http://sincityskates.com/

**Skate Attack**
http://www.skateattack.co.uk/

**Skaterbros**
http://skaterbros.com/

**Skate Buys**
http://www.skate-buys.com/

**Skates.com**
http://www.skates.com/

**Skatemall**
http://www.skatemall.com/

**Skates n Such**
http://www.skatesnsuch.com/

**Smiths Scabs**
http://www.smithsafetygear.com/

**Sure Grip**
http://www.suregrip.com/

**TSG**
http://www.ridetsg.com/

**Vanilla Skates**
http://www.vanillaskates.com/

**XSports Protective**
http://www.xsportsprotective.com/

## Useful websites
**WFTDA**
http://wftda.com/

**Two Evils**
http://www.twoevils.org/rollergirls/

**Roller Derby Worldwide**
http://www.derbyroster.com/

**Old School Derby Association**
http://osda.us/

**UK Roller Derby Association**
http://ukrda.org.uk/

**Men s Roller Derby Association**
http://www.mensderbycoalition.com/

**Derbalife**
http://derbalife.blogspot.com/

**European Roller Derby Central**
http://www.euroderby.org/

**Roller Derby Workout**
http://www.rollerderbyworkout.com/

**Roller Derby Foundation**
http://www.rollerderbyfoundation.org/

**Derby News Network**
http://www.derbynewsnetwork.com/

**Roller Derby UK TV**
http://rduk.tv/

**Rollin News**
http://rollinnews.com/

**Roller Derby Inside Track**
http://www.rollerderbyinsidetrack.com/

**Derby Deeds**
http://derbydeeds.com/

**A Bomber Nation**
http://rollerderbyradio.podbean.com/

## Blogs
**WFTDA**
http://wftda.tumblr.com/

**Kamikaze Kitten**
http://www.kamikazekitten.co.uk/KamikazeKitten/Blog/

**Yo Roller Derby**
http://www.yorollerderby.com/

**Secret Diary of a Rookie Rollergirl**
http://secretdiaryofarookierollergirl.wordpress.com/

**Derby Girls Blog**
http://derbygirlsblog.com/

**Queen of the Rink**
http://www.queenoftherink.com/

**Roller Derby Workouts**
http://rollerderbyworkouts.blogspot.co.uk/

**Jerry Seltzer**
http://jerryseltzer.wordpress.com/

**Bonnie D. Stroir**
http://livelovederby.blogspot.co.uk/

**All Derby Drills**
http://www.allderbydrills.com/

**Roller Derby Riot**
http://www.rollerderbyriot.com/blog/

## Events
**Rollercon**
http://rollercon.net/

**The Big 5 WFTDA Tournaments**
http://wftda.com/The-Big-5

**WFTDA Events**
http://wftda.com/events

**Roller Derby World Cup**
http://www.bloodandthundermag.com/WorldCup2011.htm

**Pro Roller Derby**
http://prorollerderby.com/

# Index

## Contributors' biographies

*Kamikaze Kitten* has been with London Rollergirls for four and a half years and captain of London Brawling – the number five team in the Eastern Region – for the last three seasons. She was given the honour of representing Team England MVP in the first ever Roller Derby World Cup held in Toronto in 2011. Kami believes that derby skaters should be athletes and trains hard enough for any Olympic competition, but she also loves the distinct personality that sets it apart from regular team sports.

*Suzy Hotrod* has played for Gotham Girls Roller Derby, NY for seven seasons. She is an All Star member and captain of her home team Queens of Pain. Suzy also co-captained Team USA in the Roller Derby World Cup and was featured in ESPN Magazine's The Body Issue in 2011.

*Bonnie D. Stroir* started playing roller derby for the LA Derby Dolls in 2003. She founded the San Diego Derby Dolls in 2005 and spent an equal amount of time on both flat and banked tracks blocking, jamming, coaching, skating and running the business to the best of her ability. In 2011 she 'retired' from competition to travel the world and become the sport's first full-time roller derby strategy and technique coach. She also served as assistant coach for Team USA in the 2011 Roller Derby World Cup.

## Acknowledgments

I would like to thank Lisa Thomas for making this book possible, Saffron Stocker for all her hard work designing the beautiful interiors of the book, James Watson for a brilliant cover, Jason Ruffell, Danny Bourne, Steve Brown and Amanda Renee for the fantastic photography, Suzy Hotrod, Bonnie D. Stroir and Kamikaze Kitten for their writing and inspiring contributions to the book, Reece O'Connell for very helpful sport-specific training information and Isabelle Ringer, Pitchit Davis, Lulu Demon, Red N' Roll, Kit Kat Power, Raw Heidi, Em Dash, Hyper Lynx, Miss American Thighs, Double Clutch, Molotov M. Pale, Frak Attack, Triple Shot Misto, Krissy Krash, Rat-A-Tat Kat, Pippi Strongsocking and Anais Ninja for their interviews.